MMSE-based Algorithm for Joint Signal Detection, Channel and Noise Variance Estimation for OFDM Systems

FOCUS SERIES

Series Editor Bernard Dubuisson

MMSE-based Algorithm for Joint Signal Detection, Channel and Noise Variance Estimation for OFDM Systems

Vincent Savaux
Yves Louët

WILEY

First published 2014 in Great Britain and the United States by ISTE Ltd and John Wiley & Sons, Inc.

ISTE Ltd
27-37 St George's Road
London SW19 4EU
UK

www.iste.co.uk

John Wiley & Sons, Inc.
111 River Street
Hoboken, NJ 07030
USA

www.wiley.com

Library of Congress Control Number: 2014945529

British Library Cataloguing-in-Publication Data
A CIP record for this book is available from the British Library
ISSN 2051-2481 (Print)
ISSN 2051-249X (Online)
ISBN 978-1-84821-697-6

Contents

Introduction

The wireless communications field is facing a constant increase in data-rate-consuming transmissions, due to the multitude of services and applications enabled by advanced devices. Moreover, the users expect a good reliability while demanding increasingly mobility. Figure I.1 illustrates this constant evolution for mobile communications, from the "archaic" (from the present point of view) first generation (1G) telecommunications standard in the 1980s to the fourth generation (4G) today, and the fifth generation (5G) tomorrow. This evolution is made feasible by means of a constant improvement of the networks, the devices and the embedded algorithms. In this context, this book provides an original solution improving the quality of the received signal due to a quasi-optimal channel and noise level estimation, and the detection of a multi-carrier signal in a given band.

In wireless communications, the signal is transmitted over a multipath channel. This kind of channel induces frequency fading, i.e. some holes in the signal spectrum that may be destructive for the signal. The multi-carrier modulations are a good solution for fighting against this fading, since the data is spread into a large number of subcarriers in a given channel. Among them, the orthogonal frequency division multiplexing (OFDM) is widely used in a large number of standards for wireless communications (e.g. Digital Video Broadcasting (DVB) [ETS 04] or Wireless Fidelity (Wi-Fi) IEEE 802.11) and for wired communications (e.g. digital subscriber line (xDSL)) as well. This craze for OFDM is mainly due to the fact that a simple one-tap-per-carrier equalization can be performed at the receiver to invert the channel and limit the errors in the transmitted signal. Thus, the equalization performance is directly linked to the accuracy of the channel estimation. That is why the channel estimation process plays a key role in the performance of any wireless communication system.

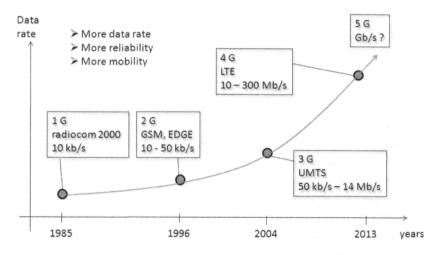

Figure I.1. *Evolution of the mobile communications from the 1G to 4G and beyond*

The linear minimum mean square error (LMMSE) method [EDF 98] is the optimal channel estimator in the sense of the mean square error. However, its practical implementation is limited since it requires the second-order moments of the channel and the noise knowledge, which are *a priori* unavailable at the receiver side. The algorithm originally proposed in [SAV 12, SAV 13a] and detailed in this book solves this problem by iteratively estimating the noise level and the channel frequency response, each parameter feeding the estimation process of the other parameter. In addition to the estimation, the proposed technique allows the receiver to detect the presence and absence of an OFDM signal in a given band. In the present wireless communication networks, the opportunistic spectrum access enabled by an accurate free-band detection seems to be a very promising solution to the increase in data rate-consuming transmissions. Thus, the proposed algorithm performs two key roles at the receiver side of an OFDM transmission. For a practical implementation, it results in a benefit in terms of space in the device, complexity and, thus, energy consumption.

This book is organized into three chapters. Chapter 1 is a background in which the system model is presented, and some basics concerning the channel statistics and the transmission of an OFDM signal over a mutlipath channel are recalled. In Chapter 2, the proposed iterative algorithm for the noise variance and the channel estimation is detailed. Two cases are considered: an ideal case in which the channel covariance matrix is supposed to be known at the receiver as originally presented in [SAV 12] and a realistic case in which this matrix is estimated as in [SAV 13a]. In Chapter 3, an application of the algorithm for the free-band detection is proposed. In both Chapters 2 and 3, the principle of the algorithm is presented in a simple way, and more elaborate developments (e.g. the proofs of convergence and the theoretical probability density functions) are also provided. The different assumptions and assertions in the developments and the performance of the proposed method are validated through simulations, and compared to methods of the scientific literature.

Background and System Model

In this first chapter, some basics regarding the propagation channel and the wireless transmission of an orthogonal frequency division multiplexing (OFDM) signal are recalled. Moreover, a brief state of the art of the pilot aided channel estimation methods is provided. Although the latter cannot be exhaustive, it covers some relevant techniques, in particular in an OFDM context.

1.1. Channel model

1.1.1. *The multipath channel*

The transmission channel (or propagation channel) is the environment situated between the transmitting and the receiving antennas. Whether an indoor or outdoor environment is considered, the signal transmitted over the channel suffers from some perturbations of different kinds: reflection, diffraction or diffusion. These phenomena are due to obstacles in the propagation environment, like buildings or walls. Besides, the transmitter, the receiver or both of them may be in motion, which induces Doppler effect.

In certain contexts, the transmitter and the receiver are in line of sight (LOS), so the channel is not destructive for the signal. On the contrary, in non-line of sight (NLOS) transmissions, the signal goes through several paths before reaching the receiving antenna. In that case, the propagation environment is called a multipath channel, and is mathematically written as a sum of weighted delayed Dirac impulses $\delta(\tau)$:

$$h(t, \tau) = \sum_{l=0}^{L-1} h_l(t)\delta(\tau - \tau_l), \qquad\qquad [1.1]$$

where the channel impulse response (CIR) $h(t, \tau)$ depends on the number of paths L, the complex gains h_l and the delays τ_l. In this work, we will instead take an interest in NLOS transmissions. The channel frequency response (CFR) is obtained from [1.1] by means of the Fourier transform (FT) operation denoted by FT:

$$H = FT_\tau(h)$$

$$H(t, f) = \sum_{l=0}^{L-1} h_l(t)e^{-2j\pi f\tau_l}, \qquad\qquad [1.2]$$

where the subscript in $FT_{(.)}$ denote the variable on which the Fourier transform is processed. Figure 1.1 illustrates this relationship ((a): $h(t, \tau)$, and (b): $H(t, f)$). We can observe that the FT is made on the delay τ, which makes the frequency response $H(t, f)$ a time-varying function. When the channel does not vary, it is called static, and when the variations are very slow, the channel is called quasi-static. In this book, we will assume the latter scenario.

1.1.2. *Statistics of the channel*

1.1.2.1. *Rayleigh channel*

As numerous natural phenomena, the transmission channel is subject to random variations. Therefore, the instantaneous CIR [1.1] and CFR [1.2] are not sufficient to completely describe the channel. It becomes relevant to use the statistical characterization of the CIR and the CFR to study this random process.

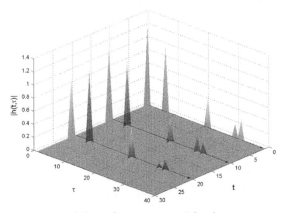

a) Impulse response $h(t, \tau)$

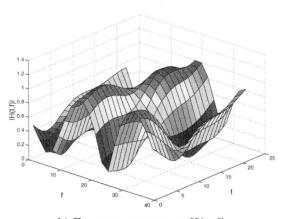

b) Frequency response $H(t, f)$

Figure 1.1. *Illustration of a time-varying impulse response $h(t, \tau)$ and a frequency response $H(t, f)$ of a multipath channel. For a color version of the figure, see www.iste.co.uk/savaux/mmse.zip*

In an NLOS transmission, due to the channel, the signal comes from all possible directions at the receiving antenna that is assumed to be isotropic. Thus, each delayed version of the received signal is considered as an infinite sum of random components. By applying the central limit theorem, $h(t)$ is then a zero-mean Gaussian complex process whose gain $|h(t)|$ follows a Rayleigh distribution [PAT 99] $p_{r,Ray}(r)$ of variance $\sigma_h^2 = E\{|h(t)|^2\}$:

$$p_{r,Ray}(r) = \frac{r}{\sigma_h^2} e^{\frac{-r^2}{2\sigma_h^2}}, \tag{1.3}$$

where r is a positive real value. The probability density function (PDF) of the phase of a Rayleigh process follows a uniform distribution, noted $p_{\phi,Ray}(\theta)$:

$$\forall \theta \in [-\pi, \pi], \ p_{\phi,Ray}(\theta) = \frac{1}{2\pi}. \tag{1.4}$$

The Rayleigh channel model is very frequently used, particularly in theoretical studies, since it is relatively close to reality, and the literature on Rayleigh distribution is very extensive. For these reasons, Rayleigh channels are considered all along this work. However, it does not cover all the possible scenarios: in a LOS context, the direct path adds a constant component to the previous model. In that case, $|h(t)|$ follows a Rice distribution, which is described in [RIC 48]. More recently, the Weibull model [WEI 51] has been proposed in order to describe real channel measurements with more accuracy. Nakagami model [NAK 60], later generalized in [YAC 00] by the $\kappa - \mu$ distribution, is also a global model from which Rayleigh's and Rice's are particular cases.

1.1.2.2. WSSUS model

The channel being a time-frequency varying random process, it is relevant to characterize it through its first and second-order statistic moments. According to Bello's work [BEL 63], let us assume a wide sense stationary uncorrelated scattering (WSSUS) model, defined as follows:

– WSS: each path $h_l(t)$ in [1.1] is a zero mean Gaussian complex process, i.e. $E\{h_l(t)\} = 0$, $\forall t$, with $E\{.\}$ the statistical expectation. Consequently, the mean of each path is independent from the time variations. Furthermore, the time correlation function $r_{h_l}(t_1, t_2) = E\{h_l(t_1)h_l^*(t_2)\}$ can be only written with the difference $\Delta_t = t_1 - t_2$, i.e.

$$r_{h_l}(t_1, t_2) = r_{h_l}(\Delta_t). \tag{1.5}$$

Each path $h_l(t)$ of the channel is then wide sense stationary.

– US: the paths are uncorrelated, so for $l_1 \neq l_2$, we have

$$E\{h_{l_1}(t)h_{l_2}^*(t)\} = 0. \tag{1.6}$$

This model is used in the following to apply the proposed detection and channel estimation algorithm. However, it does not necessarily match the reality, so we will also study the performance of the proposed method under channel model mismatch, particularly in Chapter 3.

Let us also define two very useful statistical functions that characterize the channel along the delay and the frequency axes:

– The intensity profile $\Gamma(\tau)$. A commonly used model is the decreasing exponential [EDF 98, STE 99, FOE 01].

– The frequency correlation function of the channel $R_H(\Delta_f)$, whose expression will be detailed later.

These two functions are linked by Fourier transform:

$$\Gamma = FT_{\Delta_f}^{-1}(R_H)$$
$$\Leftrightarrow R_H = FT_\tau(\Gamma). \tag{1.7}$$

Figure 1.2 depicts the decreasing intensity profile and the real and imaginary parts of the frequency correlation function.

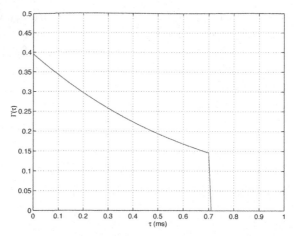

a) Channel Intensity profile $\Gamma(\tau)$.

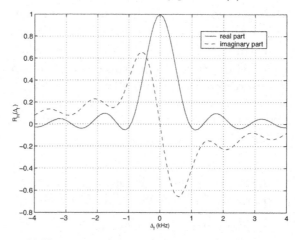

b) Frequency Correlation Function $R_H(\Delta_f)$.

Figure 1.2. *Link between the channel intensity profile and the frequency correlation function*

1.2. Transmission of an OFDM signal

When combined with a channel coding, the transmission of data using a frequency multiplexing is very robust against the frequency selective channels, in comparison with single-carrier modulations [SCO 99, DEB]. The use of orthogonal subcarriers has been proposed since the 1950s, in particular for military applications, but the acronym OFDM appeared in the 1980s, when the evolution of the technology of semiconductors enabled a great development of the implementation of complex algorithms, especially the algorithms based on large size FFT/IFFT. This kind of modulation is now used in a large number of wired and wireless transmission standards.

1.2.1. *Continuous representation*

In the continuous formalism, the baseband OFDM signal is written as:

$$s(t) = \sum_{n \in \mathbb{Z}} s_n(t) = \sqrt{\frac{1}{T_s}} \sum_{n \in \mathbb{Z}} \sum_{m=0}^{M-1} C_{m,n} \Pi(t - nT_s) e^{2j\pi m F_s t}, \qquad [1.8]$$

where $s_n(t)$ is the nth OFDM symbol, $\Pi(t)$ is the rectangular function of duration T_s as

$$\Pi(t) = \begin{cases} 1 & \text{if } -\frac{T_s}{2} \le t < \frac{T_s}{2} \\ 0 & \text{else,} \end{cases} \qquad [1.9]$$

where $F_s = \frac{1}{T_s}$ is the subcarrier spacing, M is the number of subcarriers such as, if we denote by B the bandwidth, we have $F_s = B/M$. The scalar $C_{m,n}$ with $m = 0, 1, ..., M-1$ are the information symbols coming from a set Ω of a given constellation, such as the binary phase shift keying (BPSK) or the four-quadrature amplitude modulation (4-QAM). The different subcarriers of the OFDM symbols are orthogonally arranged, thus, no interference occurs in the frequency domain (see Figure 1.3). The received signal $u(t)$ is the convolution of $s(t)$ and $h(t)$, plus the white Gaussian noise denoted by $w(t)$. In the frequency domain, due to the Fourier transform property, the convolution becomes a simple product:

$$u(t) = (h \star s)(t) + w(t) \qquad\qquad [1.10]$$

$$\overset{FT}{\Longrightarrow} U(f) = H(f).C(f) + W(f). \qquad\qquad [1.11]$$

So as to cancel the intersymbol interferences (ISIs) due to the delayed paths of the channel, the solution consists of adding a guard interval (GI) at the head of each OFDM symbol. If the GI length is greater than the maximum delay of the channel, it contains all the interferences from the previous symbol, and the GI removal cancels the ISI. In the following, let us assume that the GI is a cyclic prefix, i.e. the end of each OFDM symbol is copied at its head. As noted later, in addition to the ISI cancellation, the use of a CP gives a cyclic structure to the OFDM symbols. Let us denote by T_{CP} the duration of the CP.

Figure 1.3 shows the effects of the channel on the OFDM signal in the time and the frequency domains. Figure 1.3(a) illustrates, in the time domain, the ISI cancellation due to the CP removal. The frequency orthogonality is displayed in Figure 1.3(b). The robustness of the OFDM against the multipath channel lies in the fact that, by considering a sufficiently small intercarrier spacing F_s, one can assume that the channel is flat on each subcarrier. Consequently, a simple division per subcarrier is processed to recover the data that has been transmitted. As a matter of fact, this property is ensured when the receiver is perfectly synchronized with the signal. That will be assumed in most of the further developments. However, we will study the effect of a synchronization mismatch on the performance of the proposed detector.

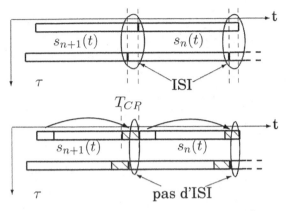

a) ISI cancellation thanks to the cyclic prefix.

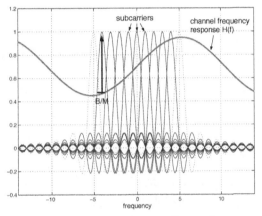

b) Frequency orthogonality between subcarriers, and effect of the channel frequency response.

Figure 1.3. *Time and frequency properties of the OFDM with cyclic prefix. For a color version of the figure, see www.iste.co.uk / savaux / mmse.zip*

1.2.2. *Discrete representation*

The orthogonal parallel subcarriers of the OFDM signal naturally leads to a discrete representation of the signal. Moreover, we perform a digital signal processing, and the discrete version of the FT, called discrete Fourier transform

(DFT), allows a generation of the OFDM symbols with a low computation cost. Note that, when the DFT size is a power of two, a fast Fourier transform (FFT) algorithm can be performed. In the discrete formalism, the use of the CP transforms the linear convolution [1.11] into a cyclic convolution [PEL 80] and, after the CP removal, the nth received OFDM symbol is then given by

$$
\mathbf{u}_n =
\begin{pmatrix}
h_{0,n} & 0 & \cdots & & \cdots & h_{L-1,n} & \cdots & h_{1,n} \\
h_{1,n} & h_{0,n} & 0 & \ddots & & \ddots & \ddots & \vdots \\
\vdots & \ddots & \ddots & & & \ddots & \ddots & h_{L-1,n} \\
h_{L-1,n} & \ddots & \ddots & h_{0,n} & 0 & \ddots & & 0 \\
0 & \ddots & \ddots & & \ddots & \ddots & & \vdots \\
\vdots & \ddots & \ddots & & & \ddots & \ddots & 0 \\
0 & \cdots & 0 & h_{L-1,n} & \cdots & h_{1,n} & h_{0,n}
\end{pmatrix}
\begin{pmatrix}
s_{0,n} \\
s_{1,n} \\
\vdots \\
\vdots \\
s_{M-1,n}
\end{pmatrix}
+ \mathbf{w}_n
$$

$$
= \underline{\mathbf{h}}_n \mathbf{s}_n + \mathbf{w}_n, \tag{1.12}
$$

where $\underline{\mathbf{h}}_n$ is the $M \times M$ circulant matrix of the channel, $\mathbf{s}_n$ is the $M \times 1$ vector containing the samples of the symbol $s_n(t)$, and $\mathbf{w}_n$ is the noise vector of size $M \times 1$. The circulant matrices are diagonalizable in the Fourier basis (see [GRA 06, CON]), whose matrix $\underline{\mathcal{F}}$ is given by

$$
\underline{\mathcal{F}} = \frac{1}{\sqrt{M}}
\begin{pmatrix}
1 & 1 & 1 & \cdots & 1 \\
1 & \omega & \omega^2 & \cdots & \omega^{(M-1)} \\
1 & \omega^2 & \omega^4 & \cdots & \omega^{2(M-1)} \\
\vdots & \vdots & \vdots & \ddots & \vdots \\
1 & \omega^{(M-1)} & \omega^{2(M-1)} & \cdots & \omega^{(M-1)^2}
\end{pmatrix},
\tag{1.13}
$$

with $\omega = e^{-\frac{2j\pi}{M}}$. It can be noticed that $\underline{\mathcal{F}}$ is an orthonormal matrix, i.e. $\underline{\mathcal{F}}\underline{\mathcal{F}}^H = \underline{\mathbf{I}}$, where $\underline{\mathbf{I}}$ is the identity matrix and H is the Hermitian transpose (or conjugate transpose). To get the frequency samples of the received signal, we calculate the

DFT of $\mathbf{u}_n$ by $\mathbf{U}_n = \mathcal{F}\mathbf{u}_n$. The matrix $\underline{\mathbf{h}}_n$ being diagonal in the Fourier basis, we simplify to get:

$$\begin{aligned} \mathbf{U}_n &= \mathcal{F}\underline{\mathbf{h}}_n\mathcal{F}^H\mathcal{F}\mathbf{s}_n + \mathbf{W}_n \\ &= \mathcal{F}\underline{\mathbf{h}}_n\mathcal{F}^H\mathbf{C}_n + \mathbf{W}_n \\ &= \underline{\mathbf{H}}_n\mathbf{C}_n + \mathbf{W}_n, \end{aligned} \qquad [1.14]$$

where $\mathbf{C}_n = \mathcal{F}\mathbf{s}_n$ is the $M \times 1$ vector containing the data $C_{m,n}$. The diagonal matrix $\underline{\mathbf{H}}_n$ is composed of the samples $H_{m,n}$ of the frequency response that is the DFT of the CIR:

$$\begin{aligned} H_{m,n} &= \sum_{l=0}^{L-1} h_{l,n} e^{-2j\pi f_m \beta_l \tau_s} \\ &= \sum_{l=0}^{L-1} h_{l,n} e^{-2j\pi \frac{m}{M}\beta_l}, \end{aligned} \qquad [1.15]$$

where $f_m = \frac{m}{M\tau_s}$ and $\beta_l = \frac{\tau_l}{\tau_s}$ sampled versions of f and τ_l, with τ_s the sampling time. Since $\underline{\mathbf{H}}_n$ is a diagonal matrix, it is usual to find an equivalent expression to [1.14]:

$$\begin{aligned} \mathbf{U}_n &= \underline{\mathbf{H}}_n\mathbf{C}_n + \mathbf{W}_n \\ \Leftrightarrow \mathbf{U}_n &= \underline{\mathbf{C}}_n\mathbf{H}_n + \mathbf{W}_n, \end{aligned} \qquad [1.16]$$

where $\underline{\mathbf{C}}_n$ is the diagonal matrix containing the samples of the vector $\mathbf{C}_n$. Moreover, each sample of $\mathbf{U}_n$ can be written as a simple scalar factor

$$U_{m,n} = H_{m,n}C_{m,n} + W_{m,n}. \qquad [1.17]$$

This shows that if the CP is well sized, it fully cancels the ISI and each transmitted symbol $C_{m,n}$ is only corrupted by the channel frequency coefficient $H_{m,n}$ and the noise $W_{m,n}$. This expression is widely exploited for the channel estimation, which will be discussed further in this work.

1.2.3. *Discrete representation under synchronization mismatch*

In [1.14], the receiver is supposed to be synchronized with the transmitted signal. In practice, the observation window of the receiver may not match the OFDM symbol, as illustrated in Figure 1.4. We then define δ the time shift. In that case, we rewrite the transmission equation [1.14] by taking into account the interference $\mathbf{I}(\delta)$ induced by δ:

$$\mathbf{U}_n = \underline{\mathbf{H}}_n \mathbf{C}_n + \mathbf{I}(\delta) + \mathbf{W}_n, \qquad\qquad [1.18]$$

where $\mathbf{I}(\delta)$ is the sum of an intercarrier interference term $\mathbf{I}^c(\delta)$ and an ISI term $\mathbf{I}^s(\delta)$. The former is due to the loss of the cyclic property implying a loss of orthogonality between the subcarriers; the latter is due to the several samples coming from the adjacent OFDM symbols.

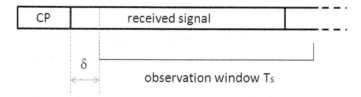

Figure 1.4. *Synchronization mismatch δ between the received signal and the observation window*

Although the receiver will be considered to be perfectly synchronized with the signal in Chapter 2, the synchronization mismatch will be taken into account to characterize the detector performance in Chapter 3.

1.3. Pilot symbol aided channel and noise estimation

1.3.1. *The pilot arrangements*

Among the wide range of channel and noise estimation techniques, we here focus on the one called "pilot symbol aided method" (PSAM) or "data aided estimation" (DAE). The pilots are particular subcarriers whose gain, phase and arrangement in the OFDM frame are known from the transmitter and the receiver. The pilot pattern depends on the time and frequency selectivity of the channel. As recalled in [OZD 07], in order to capture all the variations of the channel, the pilot gaps over the frequency axis D_p and the time axis D_t must respect the Nyquist sampling theorem:

$$D_p \leq \frac{1}{\tau_{L-1}F_s},$$
[1.19]

and

$$D_t \leq \frac{1}{2f_{D,max}T_s},$$
[1.20]

where $f_{D,max}$ is the maximum Doppler frequency. Figure 1.5 shows two usually considered arrangements in theoretical studies: (a) the block-type arrangement (also called preamble) and (b) the comb-type arrangement. The first arrangement is adapted to quasi-static channels with high-frequency selectivity. On the contrary, the comb-type arrangement (2) is used when the channel is time selective and with a low-frequency selectivity. Since we consider quasi-static channel, we will use the block-type pilot pattern.

In practical applications, such as in digital TV transmission with the digital video broadcasting-terrestrial (DVB-T) [ETS 04] standard, digital radio with the digital radio mondiale (DRM) [ETS 09] standard, or Wi-Fi [IEE 07], scattered pilots are rather considered. In that case, less subcarriers are dedicated to the channel estimation, which improves the data rate compared to the patterns of Figure 1.5, with almost the same performance.

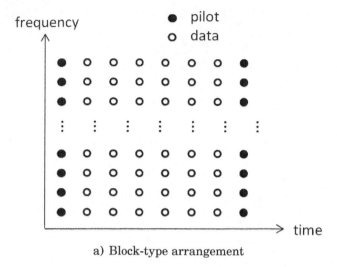

a) Block-type arrangement

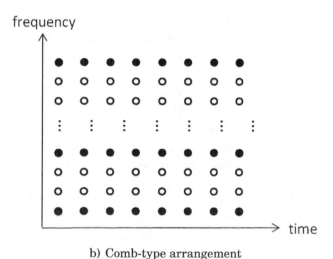

b) Comb-type arrangement

Figure 1.5. *Two possible pilot arrangements in the OFDM frame*

Whatever the pattern, we can see in Figure 1.5 that if the channel is known on the pilot tones' position, an interpolation is required to estimate the channel on all the positions of the time and frequency lattice. Some of channel estimation techniques are presented below.

1.3.2. *Channel estimation*

In the following, the developments are performed on a preamble scheme, although the results remain valid if the tones are sparsely distributed in the OFDM frame. First we detail the least square (LS) and the linear minimum mean square error (LMMSE) methods, because they are the most used and studied, and the technique proposed in this work is based on LMMSE. Second, we cover some of usual other techniques. For a clarity purpose, the subscript n is removed in the further equations.

1.3.2.1. *LS estimation*

The LS criterion aims to minimize the cost function J_{LS} that is defined as the square absolute value of the difference between the vector of the received signal $\mathbf{U}$ and the product of the transmitted signal vector $\mathbf{C}$ by a diagonal matrix $\underline{\mathbf{D}}$ whose coefficients have to be optimized. Then we get the estimation $\hat{\mathbf{H}}^{LS} = \underline{\mathbf{D}}_{opt}$. The cost function is first expressed as

$$J_{LS} = |\mathbf{U} - \underline{\mathbf{D}}\mathbf{C}|^2. \qquad [1.21]$$

Let us define the optimal matrix $\underline{\mathbf{D}}_{opt} = \hat{\underline{\mathbf{H}}}^{LS}$, where $\hat{\underline{\mathbf{H}}}^{LS}$ is the LS estimation of the CFR. After some mathematical developments, minimizing J_{LS} leads to

$$\hat{H}_m^{LS} = \frac{U_m}{C_m} = H_m + \frac{W_m}{C_m}, \qquad [1.22]$$

namely, in a matrix form:

$$\hat{\mathbf{H}}^{LS} = \mathbf{U}\underline{\mathbf{C}}^{-1} = \mathbf{H} + \mathbf{W}\underline{\mathbf{C}}^{-1}. \tag{1.23}$$

From [1.23], it can be seen that the LS estimation is very sensitive to the noise level. To reduce the sensitivity to the noise, [BIG 04] proposes the scaled LS (SLS) estimator, in which $\hat{\mathbf{H}}^{LS}$ is multiplied by a coefficient γ, which is chosen such as the mean square error $E\{||\mathbf{H} - \gamma\hat{\mathbf{H}}^{LS}||_F^2\}$ is minimized, with $||.||_F$ the Frobenius norm[1]

1.3.2.2. *LMMSE estimation*

The LMMSE aims to minimize the cost function defined by the mean square error of the error vector $\mathbf{H} - \underline{\mathbf{D}}\mathbf{U}$, as shown in [KAY 03b]:

$$J_{LMMSE} = E\{||\mathbf{H} - \underline{\mathbf{D}}\mathbf{U}||_F^2\}, \tag{1.24}$$

where $\underline{\mathbf{D}}$ is the matrix whose coefficients have to be optimized. The LMMSE channel estimation is then given by $\hat{\mathbf{H}}^{LMMSE} = \underline{\mathbf{D}}_{opt}\mathbf{U}$. The development of [1.24] yields:

$$\begin{aligned}
\hat{\mathbf{H}}^{LMMSE} &= \underline{\mathbf{D}}_{opt}\mathbf{U} \\
&= \underline{\mathbf{R}}_H(\underline{\mathbf{R}}_H + (\underline{\mathbf{C}}\underline{\mathbf{C}}^H)^{-1}\sigma^2\underline{\mathbf{I}})^{-1}\underline{\mathbf{C}}^{-1}\mathbf{U} \\
&= \underline{\mathbf{R}}_H(\underline{\mathbf{R}}_H + (\underline{\mathbf{C}}\underline{\mathbf{C}}^H)^{-1}\sigma^2\underline{\mathbf{I}})^{-1}\hat{\mathbf{H}}^{LS},
\end{aligned} \tag{1.25}$$

where $\underline{\mathbf{R}}_H = E\{\mathbf{H}\mathbf{H}^H\}$ is the channel covariance matrix. LMMSE is, by definition, the optimal estimator in the sense of the mean square error. However, we notice in [1.25] that LMMSE has two main drawbacks: first, LMMSE is far more complex than LS, due to the matrix inversion and

---

1 The matrix Frobenius norm of a matrix $\underline{\mathbf{A}}$ is defined by $||\underline{\mathbf{A}}||_F = \sqrt{tr(\underline{\mathbf{A}}\mathbf{A}^H)}$.

multiplication. Second, LMMSE requires the second-order moments of the channel $\mathbf{R}_H$ and of the noise σ^2, which are *a priori* unknown. The algorithm detailed in this book has been originally proposed to address this latter drawback, by iteratively estimating the noise level and the channel by means of the MMSE criterion.

1.3.2.3. *Other estimation techniques*

Due to the LS estimator, the noisy CFR is obtained on the pilot tones. In numerous cases, an interpolation is then required to estimate the channel on the whole subcarriers of the time and frequency lattice. A very wide range of estimation methods is described in the literature, so it is impossible to draw up an exhaustive list, but around 20 of the most used techniques are described in [HSI 98, JAF 00, MOR 01, COL 02, SHE 06, DON 07]. Among them, we will cite the 2D Wiener filter, described in [HOE 97], which is the generalized form of the optimal LMMSE estimator over the two-dimensions time and frequency. However, its practical implementation is limited by its very high computation cost. Far more simple, the interpolated fast Fourier transform (iFFT) (do not mistake for inverse FFT) [SCH 92, LE 07] is a very usual interpolation method in signal processing. After having performed the LS estimation on the pilot subcarriers, the estimated CIR is computed by means of an IFFT. Then, some zeros are added at the end of the estimated IR vector (zero padding) and finally, an FFT is done to get the estimated CFR. As mentioned in [SCH 92], the iFFT channel estimation suffers from the leakage that is induced in the adjacent channel. Another usual estimator, called maximum likelihood (ML) and described in [KAY 03a, ABU 08], aims to minimize the cost function J_{ML}:

$$J_{ML} = \ln(p(\mathbf{U}_n|\mathbf{H}_n, \underline{\mathbf{C}}_n, \sigma^2)), \qquad [1.26]$$

where $p(\mathbf{U}_n|\mathbf{H}_n, \underline{\mathbf{C}}_n, \sigma^2)$ is the conditional PDF of the received signal. As indicated in [WIE 06], in the case of a preamble, maximizing J_{ML} is exactly equivalent to minimizing J_{LS} in [1.21]. ML becomes very useful when the number of pilots is lower than the FFT size, even though, in that case, the maximization of J_{ML} has a very high calculation cost. To reduce this complexity, the expectation-maximization (EM) algorithm was originally proposed in 1977 by Dempster *et al.* in [DEM 77]. This is an iterative algorithm whose performance tends to that of the MLs when the iterations number increases.

Some interpolation methods based on polynomials are also commonly used in practical implementations. Indeed, they are more simple than the previous methods, and do not require any knowledge of the channel or signal statistics. In particular, we can cite:

– The nearest-neighbor (NN) interpolation is the most simple as it uses a polynomial of degree zero. Thus, for a given frequency position f near a pilot position f_p, the NN interpolator is expressed by:

$$\hat{H}(f) = \hat{H}(f_p). \tag{1.27}$$

Despite its simplicity, it is obvious that this method is only adapted for channel that are very weakly selective.

– The linear interpolation uses polynomials of degree one. Thus, for a value $f \in [f_p, f_{p+\delta_f}]$, where δ_f is the gap between two consecutive pilots, the estimated channel $\hat{H}(f)$ is expressed by

$$\hat{H}(f) = \hat{H}(f_p) + (f - f_p)\frac{\hat{H}(f_{p+\delta_f}) - \hat{H}(f_p)}{f_{p+\delta_f} - f_p}. \tag{1.28}$$

In the same way as the NN interpolation, this method is not accurate when the channel is highly frequency selective.

– The polynomial interpolation consists of approximating the channel $H(f)$ by a polynomial of degree $P - 1$, with P the number of pilot tones in an OFDM symbol. If a Lagrange polynomial basis $\{\mathcal{L}_0, \mathcal{L}_1, ..., \mathcal{L}_{P-1}\}$ is used, the interpolated channel is written as:

$$\hat{H}(f) = \sum_{p=0}^{P-1} \mathcal{L}_p(f)\hat{H}(f_p). \qquad [1.29]$$

The polynomial interpolation with Lagrange basis is limited by the Runge effect that results in a divergence of the estimated values between the nodes f_p when P increases. A solution consists of splitting the whole interval into several consecutive intervals containing four nodes. An interpolation of degree three is then applied in each subinterval. This solution, called piecewise cubic interpolation, is widely used. However, the interpolated channel considering the whole bandwidth B is not continuous, since cubic polynomials are concatenated. To get a continuous function, it is possible to perform the interpolation method called spline. This technique, using a Hermite polynomial basis, imposes a condition on the first derivative of the interpolated function that makes it continuous on each node.

1.3.3. *Noise variance estimation*

In addition to the multipath channel, the noise is one of the main source of disturbance for the transmitted signal. The noise is often characterized either by its power (or variance), or by the signal-to-noise ratio (SNR), i.e. by comparison with the signal level. This measurement can then be used for the design of the transmitter and the receiver. For instance, at the transmitter side, the constellation type and its size can be updated according to the SNR level [KEL 00]. At the receiver side, many algorithms such as the turbo-decoder [SUM 98] or the LMMSE channel estimation (see [1.25], [VAN 95]) require the knowledge of the SNR. We are particularly interested by the latter application in this work, since the estimator in Chapter 2 iteratively estimates the channel and the noise variance by means of the MMSE criterion.

The SNR estimation methods are commonly based on three elementary steps:

1) The noise variance estimation $\hat{\sigma}^2$ is first performed.

2) An estimation of the transmitted signal power $\hat{P}_s$ is achieved.

3) The SNR, noted ρ is finally obtained by $\hat{\rho} = \hat{P}_s/\hat{\sigma}^2$.

Alternatively, the steps (2) and (3) are sometimes replaced by the following processing:

2) The second-order moment of the received signal is estimated by $\hat{M}_2 = \hat{P}_s + \hat{\sigma}^2$.

3) the SNR is estimated by $\hat{\rho} = \hat{M}_2/\hat{\sigma}^2 - 1$.

The main difference between the techniques of the literature lies in the way to estimate σ^2. A wide range of usual methods are described in [PAU 00, LI 02, REN 05]. Among them, the second- and fourth-order moment (M$_2$M$_4$) estimator is first mentioned in [BEN 67]. Its principle is to estimate the second-order moment of the received signal U_m as $M_2 = E\{U_m U_m^*\} = P_s + \sigma^2$ on the one hand, and the fourth-order moment $M_4 = E\{(U_m U_m^*)^2\} = P_s^2 + 4P_s\sigma^2 + 2\sigma^4$ on the other hand. Then, the signal and the noise powers estimations are deduced by:

$$\hat{P}_s = \sqrt{2\hat{M}_2^2 - \hat{M}_4} \qquad\qquad [1.30]$$

$$\hat{\sigma}^2 = \hat{M}_2 - \sqrt{2\hat{M}_2^2 - \hat{M}_4}. \qquad\qquad [1.31]$$

In [REN 05], an alternative M$_2$M$_4$ method is proposed, using a new definition of the fourth order moment $M_4' = E\{(\Re\mathfrak{e}(U_m)^2 + \Im\mathfrak{m}(U_m)^2)^2\}$, where $\Re\mathfrak{e}(.)$ and $\Im\mathfrak{m}(.)$

denote the real part and the imaginary part of a complex number, respectively. The advantages of the M_2M_4 lie in the facts that it does not require any channel estimation and that it has a low complexity. However, its efficiency is degraded if the channel is frequency selective.

The ML estimator, whose developments are given in [KAY 03b] for the noise variance estimation, supposes the channel to be known, or requires a high complexity, as previously mentioned. The minimum mean square error (MMSE) estimator

$$\hat{\sigma}^2 = \frac{1}{M} E\{\|\mathbf{U} - \mathbf{CH}\|_F^2\}, \qquad [1.32]$$

from which the method that is proposed in this work is derived, also requires the CFR, which is practically replaced by its estimated value. Thus, the performance of the MMSE estimation depends on the channel estimation. References such as [PAU 00, BOU 03, XU 05a] only derive a theoretical expression of the MMSE in which the channel is supposed to be known, but the authors do not propose any practical solution to reach it.

These usual methods can be derived in the OFDM context, as it is done by the authors of [XU 05a]. If, in addition, a frequency selective channel is considered, the literature proposes two strategies for the SNR estimation. The first strategy uses the previously cited methods, and requires a channel estimation. In the second strategy, the estimation of the CFR is avoided [BOU 03, REN 09]. In [BOU 03], the author proposes a method for a 2×2 multi input multi output (MIMO) configuration that features a two pilot-symbols preamble and assumes that the channel coefficients are invariant over two consecutive carriers. Following a similar scheme, [REN 09] also proposes a preamble-based method using two pilot symbols for the the noise variance estimation. The received symbols in the preamble are then expressed by

$\mathbf{U}_n = \underline{\mathbf{C}}_n\mathbf{H}_n + \mathbf{W}_n$ and $\mathbf{U}_{n+1} = \underline{\mathbf{C}}_{n+1}\mathbf{H}_{n+1} + \mathbf{W}_{=1}$, where $\underline{\mathbf{C}}_{n+1}\mathbf{H}_{n+1}$ is supposed to be equal to $\underline{\mathbf{C}}_n\mathbf{H}_n$. Thus, the channel estimation is avoided because the noise variance is simply estimated by:

$$\hat{\sigma}^2 = \frac{1}{2}E\{||\mathbf{U}_n - \mathbf{U}_{n+1}||^2\}. \tag{1.33}$$

Although it is an efficient method, its main drawback is the loss of data rate due to the need of a preamble composed of two pilots. This is especially the case if a preamble must be regularly inserted, as in the case of time-varying channels. In [XU 05b], the SNR is estimated by means of the properties of the channel covariance matrix. As presented in section 1.1, the channel has a length L. Thus, its covariance matrix has L non-null eigenvalues from which M_2 is estimated and $M - L$ null eigenvalues from which σ^2 is estimated. This method is limited by the channel insufficient statistics, which degrades the estimation performance.

1.4. Work motivations

This work focuses on the MMSE-based channel and noise variance estimation. As has been mentioned, LMMSE is the optimal channel estimator in the sense of the mean square error, but it requires the second-order moments of the channel and the noise to be performed (see [1.25]). However, these parameters are usually unknown at the receiver and must be estimated. The solution detailed in this work consists of feeding the LMMSE estimation by the optimal MMSE estimated noise level [1.32]. To best match the unknown CFR, we propose to replace it by its LMMSE estimated value, so it clearly appears that one estimation feeds the other estimation. As a result, it seems natural to propose an iterative algorithm for the joint estimation of the noise variance and the channel. Since we suppose no *a priori* CSI at the receiver, this algorithm is valid for communications systems such as Wi-Fi or LTE, and for broadcast systems such as DRM/DRM+ [ETS 09] or DVB-T [ETS 04] as well.

In addition to the joint noise and channel estimation, it is possible to use the proposed estimator to measure the noise level in a free band, by keeping exactly the same structure. Thus, according to a given detection test, the algorithm enables the receiver to determine if a user is in a band or not. The two different uses of the technique, estimator and detector are described in Chapters 2 and 3, respectively.

Joint Channel and Noise Variance Estimation in the Presence of the OFDM Signal

In this chapter, the algorithm is presented for two scenarios: in section 2.1, an ideal case in which the channel covariance matrix supposed to be known at the receiver side is developed. This has been originally proposed in [SAV 12, SAV 14]. Section 2.2 deals with a more realistic approach of the method detailed in [SAV 13a, SAV 13b], in which the covariance matrix is estimated. Let us recall that the channel is considered to be quasi-static, and the pilot tones are arranged in a preamble, as depicted in Figure 1.5(a).

2.1. Presentation of the algorithm in an ideal approach

2.1.1. *Channel covariance matrix*

In this section, the channel covariance matrix is assumed to be known at the receiver, and two cases are considered, according to the way it is computed:

$- \underline{\mathbf{R}}_H = \mathbf{H}\mathbf{H}^H$ is the instantaneous covariance matrix, and is called "case 1";

– $\breve{\mathbf{R}}_H$ is the covariance matrix computed by means of the statistics of the channel (see [EDF 98, SAV 13d] for more specifications):

$$(\breve{\mathbf{R}}_H)_{u,v} = \sum_{l=0}^{L-1} \int_0^{\tau_{max}} \Gamma_l(\tau) e^{-2j\pi \frac{(u-v)}{M} \tau} d\tau. \qquad [2.1]$$

It can be noted that the samples of the channel covariance matrix are the Fourier transform of the intensity profile, as written in [1.7] in the continuous formalism. LMMSE performed with $\breve{\mathbf{R}}_H$ is called "case 2" in the following. Figure 2.1 displays two commonly used intensity profile shapes: the decreasing profile, as mentioned in Chapter 1, and the constant profile. As a matter of fact, the latter usually replaces the real intensity profile to perform LMMSE with channel covariance mismatch [EDF 98]. This method is less accurate and also less complex than the perfect LMMSE.

In the following, we denote by λ_m the eigenvalues of the channel, with $n = 0, 1, .., M - 1$. Without loss of generality, the pilots and the channel are normalized, i.e. for all pilot tones $m = 0, .., M - 1$, $\mathcal{P} = C_m C_m^* = 1$ and $\frac{1}{M} \sum_{m=0}^{M-1} \lambda_m = 1$.

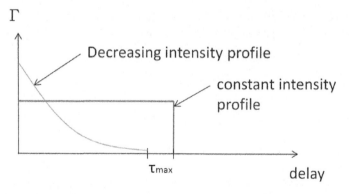

Figure 2.1. *Decreasing and constant intensity profiles* $Gamma(\tau)$

2.1.2. *MMSE noise variance estimation*

It was noted in Chapter 1 that the MMSE noise variance estimation [1.32] requires the CFR to be performed. In practice, it is replaced by the channel estimation; so the MMSE noise variance estimation is rewritten as:

$$\hat{\sigma}^2 = \frac{1}{M} E\{\|\mathbf{U} - \mathbf{C}\hat{\mathbf{H}}\|_F^2\}. \tag{2.2}$$

As it is assumed that $\mathcal{P} = 1$, then [2.2] yields:

$$\hat{\sigma}^2 = \frac{1}{M} E\{\|\mathbf{U}\mathbf{C}^{-1} - \hat{\mathbf{H}}\|_F^2\}$$

$$= \frac{1}{M} E\{\|\hat{\mathbf{H}}^{LS} - \hat{\mathbf{H}}\|_F^2\}. \tag{2.3}$$

In a more general case where $\mathcal{P} = \alpha$, we find $\hat{\sigma}^2$ from [2.3] by simply multiplying the right part of the equality by α. From the same equation, we can conclude that the higher the accuracy of the channel estimation (i.e. $\hat{\mathbf{H}}$ becoming similar to $\mathbf{H}$), the better the noise variance estimation.

2.1.3. *Proposed algorithm: ideal approach*

2.1.3.1. *Description of the algorithm*

Since the performance of the MMSE noise variance estimation in [2.3] requires an accurate channel estimation, it is proposed in [SAV 12] to use the LMMSE estimator. At the same time, the noise variance is required in this channel estimation [1.25]. As the noise variance estimation feeds the channel estimation and *vice versa*, an iterative technique allowing a joint estimation of the noise variance and the channel frequency response is proposed. The principle of the algorithm is shown in Figure 2.2.

The steps of the algorithm are given as follows and summarized below in algorithm 1. We denote by i the iteration index. The algorithm can be performed with the matrix $\underline{\mathbf{R}}_H$ as well as with $\check{\underline{\mathbf{R}}}_H$. We recall that an LS estimation of the channel is beforehand performed on the pilot tones:

1) Initialize the noise variance so that $\hat{\sigma}^2_{(i=0)} > 0$. The inequality is strict because if the initialization $\hat{\sigma}^2_{(i=0)}$ were equal to zero, the LMMSE channel estimation would be equivalent to the LS channel estimation. If the LS channel estimation were chosen to perform the noise variance estimation in [2.3], it would lead to $\hat{\sigma}^2_{(i=1)} = 0$. In this condition, the algorithm would enter an endless loop. Furthermore, fix a stopping criterion e_σ.

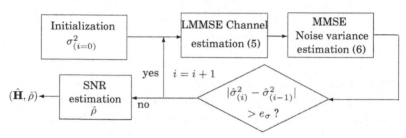

Figure 2.2. *Block diagram of the proposed iterative algorithm*

For $i \geq 1$:

2) Perform an LMMSE estimation of the channel by using

$$\hat{\mathbf{H}}^{LMMSE}_{(i)} = \underline{\mathbf{R}}_H(\underline{\mathbf{R}}_H + \hat{\sigma}^2_{(i-1)}\underline{\mathbf{I}})^{-1}\hat{\mathbf{H}}^{LS}. \qquad [2.4]$$

3) For $i \geq 1$, perform the MMSE noise variance estimation $\hat{\sigma}^2_{(i)}$ with

$$\hat{\sigma}^2_{(i)} = \frac{1}{M}E\{||\hat{\mathbf{H}}^{LS} - \hat{\mathbf{H}}^{LMMSE}_{(i)}||^2\}. \qquad [2.5]$$

4) While $|\hat{\sigma}^2_{(i)} - \hat{\sigma}^2_{(i-1)}| > e_\sigma$, go back to step 3 with $i \leftarrow i + 1$; otherwise, go to step 6.

5) Estimate the SNR $\hat{\rho}$ from the final noise variance estimation noted $\hat{\sigma}^2_{(i_f)}$:

$$\hat{\rho} = \frac{\hat{M}_2}{\hat{\sigma}^2_{(i_f)}} - 1, \qquad\qquad [2.6]$$

where (i_f) indicates the index of the last iteration.

6) End of the algorithm.

---

begin
   Initialization: $e_\sigma > 0$, $\hat{\sigma}^2_{(i=0)}$;
   $i \leftarrow 1$;
   while $|\hat{\sigma}^2_{(i)} - \hat{\sigma}^2_{(i-1)}| > e_\sigma$ **do**
      Perform an LMMSE channel estimation [2.4] ;
      Perform the noise variance estimation [2.5] ;
      $i \leftarrow i + 1$;
   end
   Estimate the SNR $\hat{\rho}$ [2.6] with $\hat{\sigma}^2_{(i_f)}$;
end

Algorithm 1. *MMSE-based joint estimation of channel and SNR, theoretical case*

Figure 2.3, which will remain valid in the realistic scenario, depicts the way in which the algorithm works. The joint estimation of $(\hat{\mathbf{H}}_{(i)}, \hat{\sigma}^2_{(i)})$ is shown in a Cartesian system. From the initialization $\hat{\sigma}^2_{(i=0)}$, the noise variance and channel estimations alternatively feed each other until the algorithm reaches its limit $(\hat{\mathbf{H}}_{i_f}, \hat{\sigma}^2_{i_f})$. Note that this couple is different from the values $(\mathbf{H}, \sigma^2)$, which characterizes the perfect estimation. This very low bias of estimation will be more precisely measured afterward.

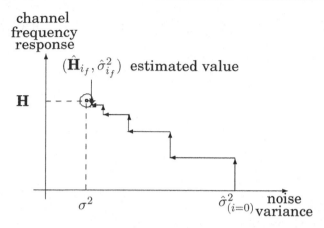

Figure 2.3. *Principle of the proposed iterative algorithm*

2.1.3.2. *Convergence of the algorithm*

Now we are going to show that the proposed algorithm converges, i.e. the noise variance $\hat{\sigma}^2_{(i)}$ and the channel frequency response $\hat{\mathbf{H}}_{n(i)}^{LMMSE}$ estimations reach a finite limit. This proof has been developed in [SAV 14]. From [2.4], it is obvious that if $(\hat{\sigma}^2_{(i)})$ admits a finite limit, $\hat{\mathbf{H}}_{(i)}^{LMMSE}$ converges to a given channel estimation. In the following, a scalar recursive expression of $\hat{\sigma}^2_{(i)}$ is derived, and then the proof of the convergence of this sequence is given.

2.1.3.2.1. Scalar expression of the sequence $(\hat{\sigma}^2_{(i)})$

In the following, the different mathematical formulations are based on the covariance matrix $\underline{\mathbf{R}}_H$. However, the developments remain valid with $\underline{\check{\mathbf{R}}}_H$ since it is also a Hermitian matrix. Since $\mathcal{P} = 1$, we have $\underline{\mathbf{C}}\underline{\mathbf{C}}^H = \underline{\mathbf{I}}$; therefore, the development of [2.5] yields

$$\hat{\sigma}^2_{(i+1)} = \frac{1}{M} E\{||\hat{\mathbf{H}}^{LS} - \hat{\mathbf{H}}^{LMMSE}_{(i+1)}||^2_F\}$$

$$= \frac{1}{M} E\{||\hat{\mathbf{H}}^{LS} - \underline{\mathbf{R}}_H(\underline{\mathbf{R}}_H + \hat{\sigma}^2_{(i)}(\mathbf{C}\mathbf{C}^H)^{-1})^{-1}\hat{\mathbf{H}}^{LS}||^2_F\}$$

$$= \frac{1}{M} E\{||\hat{\mathbf{H}}^{LS} - \underline{\mathbf{R}}_H(\underline{\mathbf{R}}_H + \hat{\sigma}^2_{(i)}\underline{\mathbf{I}})^{-1}\hat{\mathbf{H}}^{LS}||^2_F\}. \qquad [2.7]$$

By noticing that $\underline{\mathbf{R}}_H = (\underline{\mathbf{R}}_H + \hat{\sigma}^2_{(i)}\underline{\mathbf{I}}) - \hat{\sigma}^2_{(i)}\underline{\mathbf{I}}$, let us factorize [2.7] as:

$$\hat{\sigma}^2_{(i+1)} = \frac{1}{M} E\{||(\hat{\sigma}^2_{(i)}\underline{\mathbf{I}}(\underline{\mathbf{R}}_H + \hat{\sigma}^2_{(i)}\underline{\mathbf{I}})^{-1})\hat{\mathbf{H}}^{LS}||^2_F\}$$

$$= \frac{1}{M} tr \left(E\{(\hat{\sigma}^2_{(i)}(\underline{\mathbf{R}}_H + \hat{\sigma}^2_{(i)}\underline{\mathbf{I}})^{-1}\hat{\mathbf{H}}^{LS}) \right.$$

$$\left. \times (\hat{\sigma}^2_{(i)}\underline{\mathbf{I}}(\underline{\mathbf{R}}_H + \hat{\sigma}^2_{(i)}\underline{\mathbf{I}})^{-1}\hat{\mathbf{H}}^{LS})^H\} \right).$$

$$[2.8]$$

The sole random variable remaining in [2.8] is $\hat{\mathbf{H}}^{LS}$, so we get

$$\hat{\sigma}^2_{(i+1)} = \frac{1}{M} tr \left((\hat{\sigma}^2_{(i)}(\underline{\mathbf{R}}_H + \hat{\sigma}^2_{(i)}\underline{\mathbf{I}})^{-1})E\{(\hat{\mathbf{H}}^{LS}(\hat{\mathbf{H}}^{LS})^H)\} \right.$$

$$\left. \times (\hat{\sigma}^2_{(i)}\underline{\mathbf{I}}(\underline{\mathbf{R}}_H + \hat{\sigma}^2_{(i)}\underline{\mathbf{I}})^{-1}) \right)$$

$$= \frac{1}{M} tr \left(\hat{\sigma}^4_{(i)}(\underline{\mathbf{R}}_H + \hat{\sigma}^2_{(i)}\underline{\mathbf{I}})^{-1}(\underline{\mathbf{R}}_H + \sigma^2\underline{\mathbf{I}})(\underline{\mathbf{R}}_H + \hat{\sigma}^2_{(i)}\underline{\mathbf{I}})^{-1} \right).$$

$$[2.9]$$

Since $\underline{\mathbf{R}}_H$ is a Hermitian and positive semi-definite matrix, it can be diagonalized by using a unitary matrix $\mathbf{Q}$ [BIG 04, GRA 06]. Moreover, whatever $\alpha \in \mathbb{C}$, it is obvious that the matrix $\underline{\mathbf{R}}_H + \alpha\underline{\mathbf{I}}$ has the same eigendecomposition basis as $\underline{\mathbf{R}}_H$. We can deduce that $\underline{\mathbf{R}}_H + \sigma^2\underline{\mathbf{I}}$ and $\underline{\mathbf{R}}_H + \hat{\sigma}^2_{(i)}\underline{\mathbf{I}}$ are diagonalizable in the same basis, and we note:

$$\mathbf{D}_H = \mathbf{Q}^H(\mathbf{R}_H + \sigma^2\mathbf{I})\mathbf{Q}, \text{ and}$$

$$\mathbf{D}_{H(i)} = \mathbf{Q}^H(\mathbf{R}_H + \hat{\sigma}^2_{(i)}\mathbf{I})\mathbf{Q}, \tag{2.10}$$

where $\mathbf{D}_H$ and $\mathbf{D}_{H(i)}$ are diagonal matrices, whose elements are $\lambda_m + \sigma^2$ and $\lambda_m + \hat{\sigma}^2_{(i)}$, respectively. Consequently, [2.9] can be rewritten as follows:

$$\hat{\sigma}^2_{(i+1)} = \frac{1}{M}tr\left(\hat{\sigma}^4_{(i)}\mathbf{Q}(\mathbf{D}_{H(i)})^{-1}(\mathbf{D}_H)(\mathbf{D}_{H(i)})^{-1}\mathbf{Q}^{-1}\right). \tag{2.11}$$

From [2.11], we obtain a recursive formulation of $\hat{\sigma}^2_{(i+1)}$:

$$\hat{\sigma}^2_{(i+1)} = \frac{\hat{\sigma}^4_{(i)}}{M}\sum_{m=0}^{M-1}\frac{\lambda_m + \sigma^2}{(\lambda_m + \hat{\sigma}^2_{(i)})^2}. \tag{2.12}$$

From [2.12], we notice that the sequence $(\hat{\sigma}^2_{(i+1)})$ is defined by a function f_t such that if we set $x = \hat{\sigma}^2_{(i)}$, we have

$$f_t(x) = \frac{x^2}{M}\sum_{m=0}^{M-1}\frac{\lambda_m + \sigma^2}{(\lambda_m + x)^2}. \tag{2.13}$$

It can be seen that f_t is not defined for $x = 0$ because the minimum value of the eigenvalues is zero. Thus, f_t is defined for $x \in]0, +\infty]$. Furthermore, since $\sigma^2_{i=0}$ does not appear in [2.12], the sequence is independent of the initialization value.

2.1.3.2.2. Proof of convergence

The proof of the convergence of the sequence $(\hat{\sigma}^2_{(i)})$ is based on the fixed-point theorem. It is known that the sequence $(\hat{\sigma}^2_{(i+1)})$ converges if the equation

$$f_t(x) = x \tag{2.14}$$

has at least one solution, the solution being one of the fixed points of f_t. Yet, it is known that f_t has at least a fixed point on a closed interval $[a, b]$ (a and b are defined afterward) if $f_t([a, b]) \subset [a, b]$. Moreover, the sequence $(\hat{\sigma}_{(i)}^2)$ converges to one of the fixed points of f_t if it is bounded and monotonous.

We first prove that $f_t([a, b]) \subset [a, b]$. To this end, we recall that, as the channel has a length L and its covariance matrix is positive semi-definite, its eigenvalues are positive or null according to the value of m:

$$\begin{cases} \lambda_m \geq 0, & \text{if } m = 0, .., L - 1 \\ \lambda_m = 0, & \text{if } m = L, .., M - 1 \end{cases} . \tag{2.15}$$

From [2.13], we deduce the limits of f_t:

$$\lim_{x \to +\infty} f_t(x) = \frac{1}{M} \sum_{m=0}^{M-1} \lambda_m + \sigma^2 = M_2, \tag{2.16}$$

and

$$\lim_{x \to 0+} f_t(x) = \frac{1}{M} \sum_{m=L}^{M-1} \sigma^2 = \frac{M-L}{M} \sigma^2. \tag{2.17}$$

As a result, [2.17] ensures the existence of a strictly positive value ϵ such that $\epsilon \in]0, \frac{M-L}{M} \sigma^2]$ and that verifies $f_t(\epsilon) \geq \epsilon$. Furthermore, assuming $x > 0$, the second derivative of f_t, defined by

$$f_t'(x) = \frac{2}{M} \sum_{m=0}^{M-1} \frac{\lambda_m(\lambda_m + \sigma^2)x}{(\lambda_m + x)^3}, \tag{2.18}$$

is positive; therefore, f_t is a strictly increasing function. From [2.16] and [2.17], we easily know that $f_t([\epsilon, +\infty[) \subset [\epsilon, M_2]$. In addition, as f_t is a strictly increasing function that is upper bounded by M_2, it justifies the following inclusion:

$$f_t([\epsilon, M_2]) \subset [\epsilon, M_2], \qquad\qquad [2.19]$$

proving then that f_t has at least one fixed point on the closed interval $[\epsilon, M_2]$. As it has been previously shown that f_t is strictly increasing on the interval $[\epsilon, +\infty[$, the sequence $(\hat{\sigma}^2_{(i)})$ is consequently monotonous. From [2.16] and [2.17], the sequence $(\hat{\sigma}^2_{(i)})$ is also lower bounded by ϵ and upper bounded by M_2. Finally, from the fixed-point theorem, $(\hat{\sigma}^2_{(i)})$ converges to one of the fixed points of f_t. Figure 2.4 displays the shape of f_t for three values of σ^2, and is compared to $y = x$. The eigenvalues follow a exponential decreasing profile as shown in Figure 2.1. Intuitively, it seems from Figure 2.4 that f_t has a unique fixed point, which is proportional to σ^2. In the following section, a proof of this supposition is proposed.

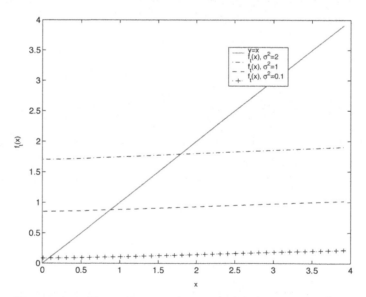

Figure 2.4. *Shape of $f_t(x)$ for three different values of σ^2, in comparison with $y = x$*

2.1.3.3. *Uniqueness of the solution: proof by contradiction*

2.1.3.3.1. Polynomial expression of the problem to solve

The function f_t is now analyzed in order to prove the uniqueness of the fixed point. A proof by contradiction is used to show the uniqueness of this solution. To do so, let us define the function g_t as

$$g_t(x) = f_t(x) - x. \qquad [2.20]$$

Let us now assume that g_t has at least two distinct solutions for the equation $g_t(x) = 0$, written down x_1 and x_2, both in $[\epsilon, M_2]$. x_1 being different from x_2, we can fix $x_2 > x_1$. Therefore, the equality $g_t(x_2) = g_t(x_1) = 0$ can be developed as

$$
\begin{aligned}
&g_t(x_2) = g_t(x_1) = 0 \\
&\Leftrightarrow \frac{1}{M}\left(\sum_{m=0}^{M-1} (\lambda_m + \sigma^2)(x_2(\lambda_m + x_1) + x_1(\lambda_m + x_2))\lambda_m \right) \\
&\quad \times \frac{\prod_{\substack{k=0 \\ k \neq m}}^{M-1}(\lambda_k + x_2)^2(\lambda_k + x_1)^2}{\prod_{m=0}^{M-1}(\lambda_m + x_2)^2(\lambda_m + x_1)^2} \\
&\quad - \frac{M \prod_{m=0}^{M-1}(\lambda_m + x_2)^2(\lambda_m + x_1)^2}{M \prod_{m=0}^{M-1}(\lambda_m + x_2)^2(\lambda_m + x_1)^2} = 0.
\end{aligned}
$$

$$[2.21]$$

It is straightforward to deduce the second line of [2.21] from the first line by dividing $g_t(x_2) = g_t(x_1) = 0$ by $x_2 - x_1$, and by taking the common denominator expression. More details are provided in [SAV 14]. The solutions of equation [2.21] are the roots of its numerator; so the study can be reduced as

$$\sum_{m=0}^{M-1} \lambda_m(\lambda_m + \sigma^2)(x_2(\lambda_m + x_1) + x_1(\lambda_m + x_2))$$

$$\times \prod_{\substack{k=0 \\ k \neq m}}^{M-1} (\lambda_k + x_2)^2(\lambda_k + x_1)^2$$

$$-M \prod_{m=0}^{M-1} (\lambda_m + x_2)^2(\lambda_m + x_1)^2 = 0$$

$$\Leftrightarrow \sum_{m=0}^{M-1} (\lambda_m(\lambda_m + \sigma^2)(x_2(\lambda_m + x_1) + x_1(\lambda_m + x_2))$$

$$-(\lambda_m + x_2)^2(\lambda_m + x_1)^2)$$

$$\times \prod_{\substack{k=0 \\ k \neq m}}^{M-1} (\lambda_k + x_2)^2(\lambda_k + x_1)^2 = 0. \qquad [2.22]$$

In order to show that f_t has a sole fixed point, it must be shown that the unique solution of [2.21] is $x_1 = x_2$. Equivalently, we show that equation [2.22] has no solution, whatever the values of x_1, x_2, λ_m and σ^2. To this end, since $\forall m = 0, 1, ..., M - 1$, $\prod_{\substack{k=0 \\ k \neq m}}^{M-1}(\lambda_k + x_2)^2(\lambda_k + x_1)^2$ is strictly positive, it is possible to reduce the study to the polynomial form P defined by

$$P(x_1, x_2, \lambda_m, \sigma^2) = \lambda_m(\lambda_m + \sigma^2)(x_2(\lambda_m + x_1) + x_1(\lambda_m + x_2))$$

$$-(\lambda_m + x_2)^2(\lambda_m + x_1)^2. \qquad [2.23]$$

If it is proved that $P(x_1, x_2, \lambda_m, \sigma^2)$ has the same sign for all $m = 0, 1, ..., M - 1$, then [2.21] has no root. Thus, the only solution of the equation $g_t(x_2) - g_t(x_1) = 0$ would be $x_2 = x_1$, which contradicts the very first assumption $x_1 \neq x_2$. The sign of the obtained polynomial is derived hereafter according to both considered channel covariance matrices.

2.1.3.3.2. Sign of the polynomial considering $\underline{\mathbf{R}}_H$

First, let us consider case 1, i.e. the channel covariance matrix is $\underline{\mathbf{R}}_H = \mathbf{HH}^H$. The rank of this matrix is the one of the vector $\mathbf{H}$, i.e. its rank is equal to 1. As a result, the $M - 1$ last eigenvalues $\lambda_1, ..., \lambda_{M-1}$ of $\underline{\mathbf{R}}_H$ are zero. In this case, for all $m = 1, ..., M - 1$, the expression of the polynomial $P(x_1, x_2, 0, \sigma^2)$ is simplified as

$$P(x_1, x_2, 0, \sigma^2) = -x_2^2 x_1^2. \qquad [2.24]$$

Since the variables x_1 and x_2 are strictly positive, it can be deduced that whatever $m = 1, ..., M - 1$, the polynomial $P(x_1, x_2, 0, \sigma^2)$ has negative values. For the non-null eigenvalue λ_0, we use straightforward physical considerations to prove that the polynomial $P(x_1, x_2, \lambda_0, \sigma^2)$ is also negative. Indeed, the channel is normalized so that

$$\frac{1}{M} \sum_{m=0}^{M-1} \lambda_m = \frac{\lambda_0}{M} = 1. \qquad [2.25]$$

Therefore, we deduce $\lambda_0 = M$, and by recalling that M is the DFT size, we have $M >> 1$. Thus, it can be reasonably supposed that a wide range of noise variance values such as $\sigma^2 << \lambda_0$ can be considered. In such conditions, we get the equivalence $P(x_1, x_2, \lambda_m, \sigma^2) \sim -\lambda_0^4 = -M^4$. We conclude that for all $m = 0, ..., M - 1$, the polynomial $P(x_1, x_2, \lambda_m, \sigma^2)$ is negative. We finally conclude that the only solution of $g_t(x_2) - g_t(x_1) = 0$ is $x_1 = x_2$, that is f_t has a sole fixed point.

2.1.3.3.3. Sign of the polynomial considering $\check{\mathbf{R}}_H$

In case 2, the channel covariance matrix $\check{\mathbf{R}}_H$ is considered. The problem is slightly more complex because the rank of $\underline{\check{\mathbf{R}}}_H$ is L. The $M - L$ last eigenvalues are null; so we naturally find again $P(x_1, x_2, 0, \sigma^2) = -x_2^2 x_1^2$ for $m = L, .., M - 1$. For the L non-null eigenvalues $\lambda_0, .., \lambda_{L-1}$, the proof is based on an empirical observation. For the need of the proof, let us consider the channel with decreasing exponential profile as described in Figure 2.1. It appears that one fixed point (for instance, x_2) of f_t is roughly proportional to σ^2 such that $x_2 = \alpha \sigma^2$. Since it is assumed that $x_1 \neq x_2$, and as x_1 and x_2 play the same role in [2.23], two scenarios can be considered: either $x_1 < x_2$ or $x_1 > x_2$. These two cases are shown in Figure 2.5, which displays the polynomial $P(\sigma^2)$ versus the SNR, for $x_2/x_1 = 10$ and $x_2/x_1 = 0.1$, and for a fixed value α equal to 0.9. Furthermore, $P(\sigma^2)$ is drawn for the lowest and the highest eigenvalues of $\underline{\mathbf{R}}_H$, that is $\lambda_0 = 10.1$ and $\lambda_{L-1} = 3.71$.

Figure 2.5(a) clearly shows that $P(\sigma^2)$ is strictly negative, whatever the value of x_2/x_1, and for the two different eigenvalues. It is reasonable to suppose that it is also valid for all the eigenvalue λ_m, $m = 0, .., L - 1$. Following these empirical assumptions, we can conclude that $P(x_1, x_2, \lambda_m, \sigma^2) < 0$ for all $m = 0, .., L - 1$, and then the only solution is $x_1 = x_2$, which proves that the fixed point of f_t is unique. It is nevertheless possible to find the scenarios that lead to the opposite observation. For instance, 2.5(b) shows $P(\sigma^2)$ drawn with $\alpha = 0.09$, $x_2/x_1 = 10$ and $\lambda_m = 3.71$. In that scenario, it is possible to get $P(x_1, x_2, \lambda_m, \sigma^2) = 0$; so it is impossible to prove that the equality [2.22] is not valid. However, it is a very particular case in which x_1 and x_2 have very low values, which would correspond to a very bad noise variance estimator. Thus, by supposing that the noise estimation is well performed, it naturally leads us to the fact that the algorithm converges to a unique solution.

2.1.3.4. *Characterization of the channel and noise estimations*

It is proposed to characterize the channel estimation by its MMSE and the noise variance estimation by its bias. The complexity of the algorithm is also provided. Let us derive the latter when the algorithm is performed with the exact covariance matrix $\underline{\mathbf{R}}_H = \mathbf{HH}^H$. The bias, denoted $B(\hat{\sigma}^2)$, is defined by

$$B(\hat{\sigma}^2) = \hat{\sigma}^2 - \sigma^2. \hspace{3cm} [2.26]$$

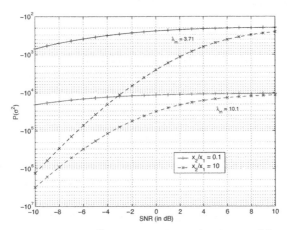

a) Shape of $P(\sigma^2)$ for two values of x_2/x_1, and for two values of λ_m

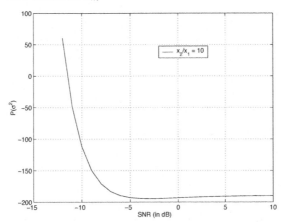

b) Shape of $P(\sigma^2)$ for $x_2 = 0.09$ of $x_2/x_1 = 10$

Figure 2.5. *Shapes of $P(\sigma^2)$ in a good and a bad scenario. For a color version of the figure, see www.iste.co.uk / savaux / mmse.zip*

When the noise variance tends to zero, we deduce from [2.13] that the sole solution of $f_t(x) = x$ is $x = 0$. Thus, the bias asymptotically tends to zero. When the algorithm reaches its limit, i.e. i tends to infinity, we have $\hat{\sigma}^2 = f_t(\hat{\sigma}^2)$. Keeping in mind that the channel covariance matrix $\mathbf{R}_H$ has rank 1 and that $\lambda_0 = M$, [2.26] is expressed by

$$
\begin{aligned}
B(\hat{\sigma}^2) &= f_t(\hat{\sigma}^2) - \sigma^2 \\
&= \frac{M-1}{M}\sigma^2 + \frac{\hat{\sigma}^4(\lambda_0 + \sigma^2)}{M(\lambda_0 + \hat{\sigma}^2)^2} \\
&= \frac{-\sigma^2(M + \hat{\sigma}^2)^2 + \hat{\sigma}^4(M + \sigma^2)}{M(M + \hat{\sigma}^2)^2}.
\end{aligned}
\tag{2.27}
$$

For a sufficiently large value of M, the bias [2.27] can be approximated by $B(\hat{\sigma}^2) \approx -\frac{\sigma^2}{M}$. We can notice that the larger the M, the higher the accuracy of the approximation. We will check the accuracy of the approximation $B(\hat{\sigma}^2) \approx -\frac{\sigma^2}{M}$ through simulation.

From the results given in [SAV 13c], we can directly give the MMSE of the LMMSE estimator when performed with noise variance mismatch:

$$
MMSE = \frac{1}{M} \frac{L^2 \hat{\sigma}^2}{L + \sum_{m=0}^{L-1} \hat{\sigma}^2 / \lambda_m}.
\tag{2.28}
$$

Since $\hat{\sigma}^2$ tends to zero when σ^2 tends to zero, we deduce that $MMSE = 0$ for $\sigma^2 = 0$. Thus, the proposed channel estimation has asymptotically the same performance as the perfect LMMSE estimator.

We give the complexity of the algorithm in terms of scalar multiplications. At each iteration, the LMMSE channel estimation [2.4] and the MMSE noise variance estimation require $2M^3$ and M operations, respectively. Overall, the algorithm requires $i_f(2M^3 + M)$ multiplications. Although it has a high complexity, the proposed technique performs a joint estimation and makes possible the LMMSE estimation without *a priori* requiring the noise variance. The computation cost can be reduced if an approximated channel covariance matrix is used [EDF 98]. Besides, it will be shown in next chapter that the proposed method enables the receiver detecting free bands in the spectrum also.

2.1.4. *Simulation results: ideal approach*

The simulations are performed using signal and channel parameters extracted from the DRM/DRM+ standard [ETS 09]. The signal features are given in Table 2.1. We recall that, according to the quasi-static transmission model, a block-type pilot arrangement as described in Figure 1.5(a) is considered to perform the estimation. The channel is based on the *US Consortium* model, whose path gains are normalized. The channel parameters are given in Table 2.2.

Robustness C	
Symbol duration	14.66 ms
CP duration	5.33 ms
Frame duration	400 ms
Number of carriers	148
Signal bandwidth	10 kHz
Signal constellation	64-QAM

Table 2.1. *Parameters of robustness C mode*

Channel model				
	path 1	path 2	path 3	path 4
delay	0 ms	0.7 ms	1.5 ms	2.2 ms
gain	0.7448	0.5214	0.3724	0.1862

Table 2.2. *Parameters of the channel model*

2.1.4.1. *Convergence of the noise variance estimation*

Figures 2.6(a) and (b) show the noise variance estimation curves in cases 1 and 2 (for $\underline{\mathbf{R}}_H$ and $\underline{\check{\mathbf{R}}}_H$, respectively) versus the number of iterations, and compare them to the exact value of the noise variance. The simulations are performed with $\rho = 0$ dB and $\rho = 10$ dB in order to show the validity of the method for any SNR values. The initialization value is first chosen to be low ($\hat{\sigma}^2_{(i=0)} = 0.1$) in Figure 2.6(a) and large ($\hat{\sigma}^2_{(i=0)} = 2$) in Figure 2.6(b). The curves are obtained after 7,000 simulation runs.

Figure 2.6 shows the convergence of the noise variance estimation, whatever the SNR and the initialization values. It validates that $(\sigma^2_{(i)})$ is monotonous, independent of the initialization value and converges to a unique solution close to the exact noise variance.

2.1.4.2. *Speed of convergence of the algorithm*

Figure 2.7 depicts the absolute difference $|\hat{\sigma}^2_{(i)} - \hat{\sigma}^2_{(i-1)}|$ versus the number of iterations starting from $i = 2$, in cases 1 and 2. Simulations are performed with the parameters $\rho = 10$ dB and the initialization value $\hat{\sigma}^2_{(i=0)} = 2$. These curves allow us to characterize the required number of iterations to get an expected threshold value e_σ.

The algorithm has a high-speed convergence. Indeed, for instance, for a given threshold $e_\sigma = 0.01$, only two iterations are needed in case 1 and three iterations are needed in case 2. Furthermore, we see in Figure 2.7 that the value of $|\hat{\sigma}^2_{(i)} - \hat{\sigma}^2_{(i-1)}|$ seems to be almost linear and it converges to zero. These results confirm the monotony and the high speed of convergence of the proposed algorithm. Consequently, it limits the complexity of the algorithm.

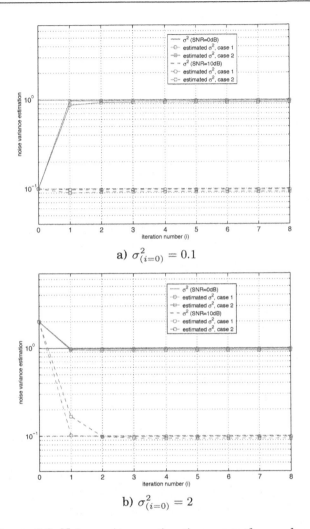

a) $\sigma^2_{(i=0)} = 0.1$

b) $\sigma^2_{(i=0)} = 2$

Figure 2.6. *Noise variance estimation versus the number of iterations in cases 1 and 2. For a color version of the figure, see www.iste.co.uk/savaux/mmse.zip*

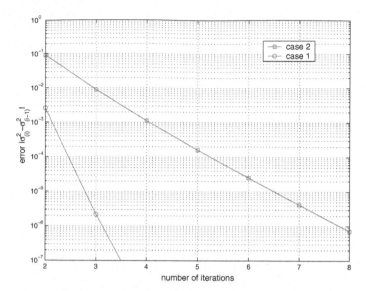

Figure 2.7. *Absolute difference between two consecutive noise variance estimations* $|\hat{\sigma}^2_{(i)} - \hat{\sigma}^2_{(i-1)}|$, *for* $\rho = 10$ *dB and* $\hat{\sigma}^2_{(i=0)} = 2$

2.1.4.3. *Bias of the noise variance estimation*

Figure 2.8 depicts the bias of the noise variance estimation $B(\hat{\sigma}^2) = \hat{\sigma}^2 - \sigma^2$ versus the FFT size when performed in case 1. We then go beyond the scope of the transmission context described in Table 2.1, since the FFT size varies from $M = 64$ to $M = 1,024$. Furthermore, $B(\hat{\sigma}^2)$ is compared to $-\frac{\sigma^2}{M}$ in order to validate the approximation $B(\hat{\sigma}^2) \approx -\frac{\sigma^2}{M}$. The curves are drawn for $\rho = 10$ dB, and the estimated bias values are obtained after averaging out 1,000 simulation runs.

We observe that the bias is non-null irrespective of the FFT size. However, this has a very low value: above -0.03 for $M = 64$ and until -0.0025 for $M = 1,024$. Furthermore, Figure 2.8 shows that the accuracy of the approximation $B(\hat{\sigma}^2) \approx -\frac{\sigma^2}{M}$ increases with M.

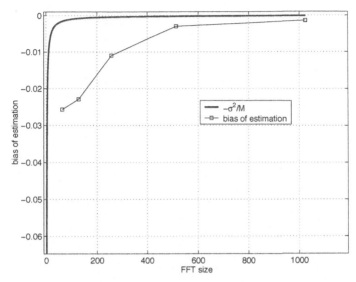

Figure 2.8. *Bias of the estimation* $B(\hat{\sigma}^2)$ *versus the FFT size in case 1, compared with* $-\frac{\sigma^2}{M}$

2.1.4.4. *Comparison of SNR estimation with other methods*

Figure 2.9 depicts the normalized mean square error (NMSE) of the SNR estimations as a function of the SNR. The proposed algorithm in cases 1 and 2 is compared to Ren's method [REN 09], Xu's method [XU 05b] and the usual M_2M_4 method. We recall that Ren's method requires two pilot symbols in order to avoid the effect of the frequency selective channel. Xu's method requires a single pilot symbol in order to compute the covariance matrix of the channel. The M_2M_4 method directly computes the SNR estimation due to the second moment-order M_2 and the fourth moment-order M_4 of the received signal. For a 16-QAM in a Rayleigh fading channel, [XU 05a] gives the estimation of the SNR as

$$\hat{\rho} = (\sqrt{M_4 - 2M_2^2})/(0.8M_2^2 - \sqrt{M_4 - 2M_2^2}). \qquad [2.29]$$

To get Figure 2.9, the initialization value is $\hat{\sigma}^2_{(i=0)} = 0.1$ and the algorithm runs until $i = 3$. The NMSE whose expression is $NMSE = E\{|\hat{\rho} - \rho|^2/\rho^2\}$ is approximated by an average on 200,000 samples.

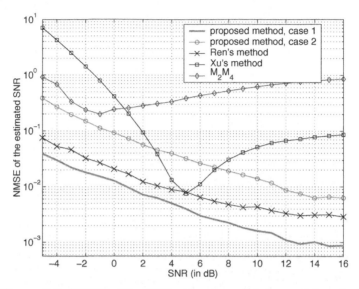

Figure 2.9. *NMSE of the SNR estimation of the proposed method compared to three existing methods. For a color version of the figure, see www.iste.co.uk / savaux / mmse.zip*

First, it can be observed that the shapes of the curves of Ren's and Xu's estimation methods match with those in [REN 09]. Second, as mentioned in [XU 05a], the performance of the M_2M_4 method is degraded in Rayleigh fading channels, which is also the case here. It can be seen that the proposed method outperforms the usual M_2M_4 method for all SNR values. The theoretical case (case 1) has a lower NMSE than the Ren's method (which outperforms Xu's method) due to the use of a perfect channel covariance matrix. In case 2, Ren's method has a lower NMSE than the proposed algorithm due to the approximation of the covariance matrix, but Ren's method requires twice as many pilot symbols. However, the proposed algorithm yields a globally lower NMSE than the Xu's method, except for SNR values between 3 and 7 dB. The Xu's method and the proposed method require only one pilot symbol; so the proposed algorithm is globally more precise for the same useful bit rate. Besides, the proposed method also performs a channel estimation, whose efficiency is studied in the next section.

2.1.4.5. *Channel estimation*

Figure 2.10 shows the bit error rate (BER) of the proposed method versus the SNR from 0 to 32 dB. Cases 1 and 2 are considered, and compared to the usual least square and the perfect estimations. The initialization noise value is set as before, i.e. $\hat{\sigma}^2_{(i=0)} = 0.1$. The BER curves are performed over 2.5×10^6 bits.

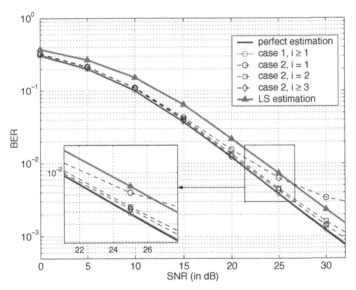

Figure 2.10. *BER versus SNR for the proposed method compared with perfect estimation and LS estimation. For a color version of the figure, see www.iste.co.uk / savaux / mmse.zip*

The simulations in Figure 2.10 show that the channel estimation converges. In case 1, the estimation reaches its limit at the first iteration, which matches the convergence speed of the noise variance estimation shown in Figure 2.9. For an SNR value equal to 25 dB, the error of case 1 compared to the perfect estimation is less than 0.1 dB. For case 2, the channel estimation reaches its limit at $i = 3$, which also tallies with the necessary iterations number to ensure that $(\hat{\sigma}^2_{(i)})$ converges. For an SNR value equal to 25 dB, the error in case 2 compared to the perfect estimation is less than 0.5 dB. Furthermore, the proposed iterative method is more efficient than the regular LS estimation. Indeed, for SNR=25 dB, the error of the LS estimation compared to the proposed method in case 2 is equal to 2.5 dB.

2.2. Algorithm in a practical approach

In this section, a scenario in which the covariance matrix is *a priori* unknown is considered. So, this case is called a realistic approach (or practical approach), in contrast with the theoretical case of the previous section. The algorithm, performed in this realistic context, has been presented in [SAV 13a, SAV 13b].

2.2.1. *Proposed algorithm: realistic approach*

In the practical case, neither the matrix $\underline{\mathbf{R}}_H$ nor $\underline{\check{\mathbf{R}}}_H$ is available at the receiver side. Thus, the channel covariance matrix must be estimated by means of the vector of the estimated channel frequency response. This estimated matrix is denoted as $\underline{\tilde{\mathbf{R}}}_H$. The algorithm, performed in this realistic case, is adapted from the one in the theoretical case. Its steps are detailed below and described in Figure 2.11, and summarized in algorithm 2.

1) At the beginning, only the LS channel estimation $\hat{\mathbf{H}}^{LS}$ is available; so, estimate the covariance matrix denoted $\underline{\tilde{\mathbf{R}}}_H^{LS}$ by

$$\underline{\tilde{\mathbf{R}}}_H^{LS} = \hat{\mathbf{H}}^{LS}(\hat{\mathbf{H}}^{LS})^H. \tag{2.30}$$

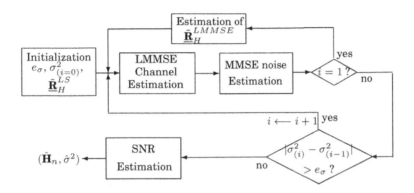

Figure 2.11. *Block diagram of the iterative algorithm in the realistic scenario*

Furthermore, fix a stopping criterion e_σ.

2) At the first step $(i = 1)$ of the algorithm, perform the LMMSE channel estimation with $\tilde{\underline{\mathbf{R}}}_H^{LS}$:

$$\hat{\mathbf{H}}_{(i=1)}^{LMMSE} = \tilde{\underline{\mathbf{R}}}_H^{LS}(\tilde{\underline{\mathbf{R}}}_H^{LS} + \hat{\sigma}_{(i=0)}^2\underline{\mathbf{I}})^{-1}\hat{\mathbf{H}}^{LS},\qquad [2.31]$$

where $\hat{\sigma}_{(i=0)}^2$ still points out the initialization value of the noise variance.

3) Estimate the noise variance in the same way as before, with $\hat{\mathbf{H}} = \hat{\mathbf{H}}_{(i=1)}^{LMMSE}$. Keeping in mind that the pilots are normalized, $\underline{\mathbf{C}}\underline{\mathbf{C}}^H$ is equal to the identity matrix $\underline{\mathbf{I}}$; therefore, it yields:

$$\hat{\sigma}_{(i=1)}^2 = \frac{1}{M}E\{||\mathbf{U} - \underline{\mathbf{C}}\hat{\mathbf{H}}_{(i=1)}^{LMMSE}||^2\}$$

$$= \frac{1}{M}E\{||\hat{\mathbf{H}}^{LS} - \hat{\mathbf{H}}_{(i=1)}^{LMMSE}||^2\}.\qquad [2.32]$$

If the algorithm keeps on computing with $\tilde{\underline{\mathbf{R}}}_H^{LS}$, Appendix 1 proves that $(\hat{\sigma}_{(i)}^2)$ converges to zero. Under this condition, the algorithm enters into an endless loop. This is due to the fact that $\tilde{\underline{\mathbf{R}}}_H^{LS}$ is sensitive to the noise. In order to obtain a more accurate channel covariance matrix, it is now possible to use $\hat{\mathbf{H}}_{(i=1)}^{LMMSE}$ such that

$$\tilde{\underline{\mathbf{R}}}_{H}^{LMMSE} = \hat{\mathbf{H}}_{(i=1)}^{LMMSE} (\hat{\mathbf{H}}_{(i=1)}^{LMMSE})^{H}. \qquad [2.33]$$

4) For $i \geq 2$, iteratively perform the estimation steps [2.31] and [2.33] by using [2.33]:

$$\hat{\mathbf{H}}_{(i)}^{LMMSE} = \tilde{\underline{\mathbf{R}}}_{H}^{LMMSE} (\tilde{\underline{\mathbf{R}}}_{H}^{LMMSE} + \hat{\sigma}_{(i-1)}^{2}\underline{\mathbf{I}})^{-1}\hat{\mathbf{H}}^{LS}, \qquad [2.34]$$

$$\hat{\sigma}_{(i)}^{2} = \frac{1}{M}E\{||\hat{\mathbf{H}}^{LS} - \hat{\mathbf{H}}_{(i)}^{LMMSE}||^{2}\}. \qquad [2.35]$$

The characterization of the initialization $\hat{\sigma}_{(i=0)}^{2}$ will be discussed later. However, it is already obvious that $\hat{\sigma}_{(i=0)}^{2}$ must be strictly positive; otherwise, $\hat{\mathbf{H}}_{(i)}^{LMMSE} = \hat{\mathbf{H}}^{LS}$ in [2.34]. In that case, $\hat{\sigma}_{(i)}^{2} = 0$, and the algorithm enters into an endless loop.

5) While $|\hat{\sigma}_{(i)}^{2} - \hat{\sigma}_{(i-1)}^{2}| > e_{\sigma}$, go back to step 4 with $i \leftarrow i+1$; otherwise, go to step 6.

6) At last, the final iteration is noted (if); estimate the SNR from the noise variance with

$$\hat{\rho} = \frac{\hat{M}_{2}}{\hat{\sigma}_{(i_f)}^{2}} - 1. \qquad [2.36]$$

7) End of the algorithm.

Note that the computation cost of the algorithm 2 slightly increases in comparison with the theoretical case. This is due to the channel covariance matrix calculation that requires M^{2} scalar multiplications. However, $\tilde{\underline{\mathbf{R}}}_{H}$ is a Hermitian matrix; therefore, its components verify $(\tilde{\underline{\mathbf{R}}}_{H})_{u,v} = (\tilde{\underline{\mathbf{R}}}_{H})_{v,u}^{*}$. Thus, the computation of the elements of the lower or upper triangle is enough to deduce the others, which reduces the complexity to $\frac{M(M+1)}{2}$.

begin

    Initialization: $\tilde{\underline{\mathbf{R}}}_H^{LS}$, $e_\sigma > 0$, $\hat{\sigma}_{(i=0)}^2$;

    $i \leftarrow 1$;

    while $|\hat{\sigma}_{(i)}^2 - \hat{\sigma}_{(i-1)}^2| > e_\sigma$ **do**

        if $i = 1$ **then**

            Perform LMMSE channel estimation [2.31] ;

            Perform the noise variance estimation [2.32] ;

            Calculate the matrix $\tilde{\mathbf{R}}_H^{LMMSE}$ [2.33] ;

        else

            Perform an LMMSE channel estimation [2.34] ;

            Perform the noise variance estimation [2.35] ;

        end

        $i \leftarrow i + 1$;

    end

    Estimate the SNR $\hat{\rho}$ [2.36] with $\hat{\sigma}_{(i_f)}^2$;

end

Algorithm 2. *MMSE-based joint estimation of both channel and SNR given in the realistic scenario*

2.2.2. *Convergence of the algorithm*

In this section, the convergence of the proposed solution is proved, when an appropriate choice of the initialization $\hat{\sigma}_{(i=0)}^2$ is done. To this end, a necessary and sufficient condition on $\hat{\sigma}_{(i=0)}^2$ is given and an optimal choice is proposed. As explained previously, if the convergence of the noise variance is proved, it is obvious that the channel estimation also converges, i.e. the algorithm converges in general.

2.2.2.1. *Scalar expression of the sequence* $(\hat{\sigma}_{(i)}^2)$

First, as was done in the previous section for the theoretical case, a scalar expression of the sequence $(\hat{\sigma}_{(i)}^2)$ is derived. Assuming $i \geq 2$ and by inserting [2.34] into [2.35], the noise variance estimation is developed as follows:

$$\hat{\sigma}^2_{(i+1)} = \frac{1}{M}E\{||\hat{\mathbf{H}}^{LS} - \hat{\mathbf{H}}^{LMMSE}_{(i+1)}||^2_F\}$$

$$= \frac{1}{M}E\{||\hat{\mathbf{H}}^{LS} - \tilde{\mathbf{R}}^{LMMSE}_H(\tilde{\mathbf{R}}^{LMMSE}_H + \hat{\sigma}^2_{(i-1)}\mathbf{I})^{-1}\hat{\mathbf{H}}^{LS}||^2_F\}$$

$$= \frac{1}{M}tr\left(\hat{\sigma}^4_{(i)}(\tilde{\mathbf{R}}^{LMMSE}_H + \hat{\sigma}^2_{(i)}\mathbf{I})^{-1}(\mathbf{R}_H + \sigma^2\mathbf{I})\right.$$

$$\left. \times (\tilde{\mathbf{R}}^{LMMSE}_H + \hat{\sigma}^2_{(i)}I)^{-1}\right). \qquad [2.37]$$

The third line of [2.37] is deduced from the second line by simply noticing that $\tilde{\mathbf{R}}^{LMMSE}_H = (\tilde{\mathbf{R}}^{LMMSE}_H + \hat{\sigma}^2_{(i-1)}\mathbf{I}) - \hat{\sigma}^2_{(i-1)}\mathbf{I}$. The matrix $\tilde{\mathbf{R}}^{LMMSE}_H$ is now expressed, assuming that it is computed after the first iteration [2.33], as

$$\tilde{\mathbf{R}}^{LMMSE}_H = \frac{1}{M}\hat{\mathbf{H}}^{LMMSE}_{(i=1)}(\hat{\mathbf{H}}^{LMMSE}_{(i=1)})^H$$

$$= (\tilde{\mathbf{R}}^{LS}_H(\tilde{\mathbf{R}}^{LS}_H + \hat{\sigma}^2_{(i=0)}\mathbf{I})^{-1}\hat{\mathbf{H}}^{LS})$$

$$\times (\tilde{\mathbf{R}}^{LS}_H(\tilde{\mathbf{R}}^{LS}_H + \hat{\sigma}^2_{(i=0)}\mathbf{I})^{-1}\hat{\mathbf{H}}^{LS})^H$$

$$= \tilde{\mathbf{R}}^{LS}_H(\tilde{\mathbf{R}}^{LS}_H + \hat{\sigma}^2_{(i=0)}\mathbf{I})^{-1}\hat{\mathbf{H}}^{LS}(\hat{\mathbf{H}}^{LS})^H$$

$$\times (\tilde{\mathbf{R}}^{LS}_H(\tilde{\mathbf{R}}^{LS}_H + \hat{\sigma}^2_{(i=0)}\mathbf{I})^{-1})^H. \qquad [2.38]$$

For a sufficiently large value of M, we consider that $\frac{1}{M}tr(\tilde{\mathbf{R}}^{LS}_H) = \frac{1}{M}tr(\mathbf{R}_H + \sigma^2\mathbf{I})$. Since the estimation of the noise variance is calculated due to the trace in [2.37], we make the assumption that, as a first approximation:

$$\tilde{\mathbf{R}}^{LS}_H = \hat{\mathbf{H}}^{LS}_p(\hat{\mathbf{H}}^{LS}_p)^H \approx \mathbf{R}_H + \sigma^2\mathbf{I}. \qquad [2.39]$$

Finally, the expression of $\tilde{\mathbf{R}}_H^{LMMSE}$ is obtained by inserting [2.39] into [2.38]:

$$\tilde{\mathbf{R}}_H^{LMMSE} = (\underline{\mathbf{R}}_H + \sigma^2\underline{\mathbf{I}})(\underline{\mathbf{R}}_H + (\sigma^2 + \hat{\sigma}^2_{(i=0)})\underline{\mathbf{I}})^{-1}(\underline{\mathbf{R}}_H + \sigma^2\underline{\mathbf{I}})$$
$$\times(\underline{\mathbf{R}}_H + (\sigma^2 + \hat{\sigma}^2_{(i=0)})\underline{\mathbf{I}})^{-1}(\underline{\mathbf{R}}_H + \sigma^2\underline{\mathbf{I}}). \quad [2.40]$$

Again, since whatever $\alpha \in \mathbb{C}$, the matrix $\mathbf{R}_H + \alpha\underline{\mathbf{I}}$ has the same eigendecomposition basis as $\mathbf{R}_H$, we can deduce that $(\underline{\mathbf{R}}_H + \sigma^2\underline{\mathbf{I}})$, $(\underline{\mathbf{R}}_H + \hat{\sigma}^2_{(i)}\underline{\mathbf{I}})$ and $\underline{\mathbf{R}}_H + (\sigma^2 + \hat{\sigma}^2_{(i=0)})\underline{\mathbf{I}}$ are diagonalizable in the same basis:

$$\underline{\mathbf{D}}_H = \underline{\mathbf{Q}}^H(\underline{\mathbf{R}}_H + \sigma^2\underline{\mathbf{I}})\underline{\mathbf{Q}},$$

$$\underline{\mathbf{D}}_{H(i)} = \underline{\mathbf{Q}}^H(\underline{\mathbf{R}}_H + \hat{\sigma}^2_{(i)}\underline{\mathbf{I}})\underline{\mathbf{Q}}, \text{ and}$$

$$\underline{\mathbf{D}}_{H(i=0)} = \underline{\mathbf{Q}}^H(\underline{\mathbf{R}}_H + (\sigma^2 + \hat{\sigma}^2_{(i=0)})\underline{\mathbf{I}})\underline{\mathbf{Q}}. \quad [2.41]$$

By substituting [2.41] into [2.40] and [2.37], and after some mathematical developments, the scalar expression of the sequence can be obtained

$$\hat{\sigma}^2_{(i+1)} = \frac{\hat{\sigma}^4_{(i)}}{M}\sum_{m=0}^{M-1}\frac{(\lambda_m + \sigma^2 + \hat{\sigma}^2_{(i=0)})^4(\lambda_m + \sigma^2)}{((\lambda_m + \sigma^2)^3 + \hat{\sigma}^2_{(i)}(\lambda_m + \sigma^2 + \hat{\sigma}^2_{(i=0)})^2)^2}$$

$$\Leftrightarrow \hat{\sigma}^2_{(i+1)} = \frac{\hat{\sigma}^4_{(i)}}{M}\sum_{m=0}^{M-1}\frac{\lambda_m + \sigma^2}{(\frac{(\lambda_m+\sigma^2)^3}{(\lambda_m+\sigma^2+\hat{\sigma}^2_{(i=0)})^2} + \hat{\sigma}^2_{(i)})^2}. \quad [2.42]$$

It can be seen that, unlike the theoretical scenario, the initialization $\hat{\sigma}^2_{(i=0)}$ appears in [2.42], and then has an influence on the convergence of the sequence. Thus, if $\hat{\sigma}^2_{(i=0)}$ is chosen close to zero, the term $\frac{(\lambda_m+\sigma^2)^3}{(\lambda_m+\sigma^2+\hat{\sigma}^2_{(i=0)})^2}$ is then roughly equal to $(\lambda_m + \sigma^2)$. In that case, Appendix 1 shows that it is equivalent to use the covariance matrix $\tilde{\mathbf{R}}_H^{LS}$ and the noise estimation then converges toward zero. The choice of the initialization will be studied later.

As mentioned previously, we can notice that the sequence $(\hat{\sigma}^2_{(i+1)})$ is built from a function, which will be denoted as f_{r2}, and if we set $x = \hat{\sigma}^2_{(i)}$, $f_{r2}(x)$ is expressed by

$$f_{r2}(x) = \frac{x^2}{M} \sum_{m=0}^{M-1} \frac{\lambda_m + \sigma^2}{\left(\frac{(\lambda_m + \sigma^2)^3}{(\lambda_m + \sigma^2 + \hat{\sigma}^2_{(i=0)})^2} + x \right)^2}. \qquad [2.43]$$

2.2.2.2. *Necessary condition for the convergence of the sequence* $(\hat{\sigma}^2_{(i)})$

In this section, a necessary condition on the initialization value $\hat{\sigma}^2_{(i=0)}$ for the convergence of the sequence $(\hat{\sigma}^2_{(i)})$ is derived. Before doing that, some properties of f_{r2} are listed here:

– Since $\frac{(\lambda_m + \sigma^2)^3}{(\lambda_m + \sigma^2 + \hat{\sigma}^2_{(i=0)})^2} > 0$, f_{r2} is continuous on $\mathbb{R}^+$.

– $\forall x \in \mathbb{R}^+$ the derivative

$$f'_{r2}(x) = \frac{2x}{M} \sum_{m=0}^{M-1} \frac{(\lambda_m + \sigma^2) \frac{(\lambda_m + \sigma^2)^3}{(\lambda_m + \sigma^2 + \hat{\sigma}^2_{(i=0)})^2}}{\left(\frac{(\lambda_m + \sigma^2)^3}{(\lambda_m + \sigma^2 + \hat{\sigma}^2_{(i=0)})^2} + x \right)^3} \qquad [2.44]$$

is positive, so f_{r2} is increasing on $\mathbb{R}^+$.

– $f_{r2}(0) = 0$.

– $\lim_{x \to \infty} f_{r2}(x) = \sum_{m=0}^{M-1} \lambda_m + \sigma^2 = M_2$.

From these four properties, we deduce the inclusion $f_{r2}([0, M_2]) \subset [0, M_2]$, and since f_{r2} is increasing on $\mathbb{R}^+$, we conclude that f_{r2} has at least one fixed point in $[0, M_2]$. From property 3, it is obvious that zero is a fixed point of f_{r2}. Since $f_{r2}(0) = 0$ and f_{r2} is increasing on $\mathbb{R}^+$, a necessary (but not sufficient) condition for f_{r2} to have other fixed points can be expressed as follows: there exists $x_0 \geq 0$ such that $\max_x(f'_{r2}(x)) = f'_{r2}(x_0) > 1$, which can allow f_2 the possibility to be above the first bisector. Then, $\hat{\sigma}^2_{(i=0)}$ can be adjusted in order to ensure this condition. If we denote $f'_{r2_m}(x)$ as the functions extracted from $f'_{r2}(x)$ such that $f'_{r2}(x) = \sum_{m=0}^{M-1} f'_{r2_m}(x)$, we have

$$f'_{r2_m}(x) = \frac{1}{M} \frac{2x(\lambda_m + \sigma^2)\frac{(\lambda_m+\sigma^2)^3}{(\lambda_m+\sigma^2+\hat{\sigma}^2_{(i=0)})^2}}{(\frac{(\lambda_m+\sigma^2)^3}{(\lambda_m+\sigma^2+\hat{\sigma}^2_{(i=0)})^2} + x)^3}.$$ [2.45]

Let us denote by $f'_{r2_{min}}(x)$ the function whose maximum reached for $x = x_{0min}$ is the lowest among all the maxima of the functions f'_{r2_m} in the set $\{f'_{r2_m}\}$, $m = 0, ..., M-1$. If we adjust $\hat{\sigma}^2_{(i=0)}$ so that $f'_{r2_{min}}(x_{0min}) \geq 1$, then we fulfill the necessary condition, $f'_{r2}(x_{0min}) \geq 1$. Indeed, if $f'_{2_{min}}(x_{0min}) \geq 1$, then

$$1 \leq f'_{r2_{min}}(x_{0min}) \leq \frac{1}{M} \sum_{m=0}^{M-1} f'_{r2_m}(x_{0min}) = f'_{r2}(x_{0min}).[2.46]$$

In order to find x_{0min}, we calculate the second derivative $f''_{r2_{min}}$ of $f_{r2_{min}}$:

$$f''_{r2_m}(x) = \frac{1}{M} \frac{2(\lambda_m + \sigma^2)\frac{(\lambda_m+\sigma^2)^3}{(\lambda_m+\sigma^2+\hat{\sigma}^2_{(i=0)})^2}(\frac{(\lambda_m+\sigma^2)^3}{(\lambda_m+\sigma^2+\hat{\sigma}^2_{(i=0)})^2} - 2x)}{(\frac{(\lambda_m+\sigma^2)^3}{(\lambda_m+\sigma^2+\hat{\sigma}^2_{(i=0)})^2} + x)^4}.$$

[2.47]

The second derivative $f''_{r2_{min}}$ is equal to zero for $x_{0min} = \frac{1}{2}\frac{(\lambda_m+\sigma^2)^3}{(\lambda_m+\sigma^2+\hat{\sigma}^2_{(i=0)})^2}$;therefore, we get the maximum value of $f'_{r2_{min}}$:

$$f'_{r2_{min}}(x_{0min}) = \frac{8}{27} \frac{(\lambda_m + \sigma^2 + \hat{\sigma}^2_{(i=0)})^2}{(\lambda_m + \sigma^2)^2}.$$ [2.48]

Whatever the values of σ^2 and $\hat{\sigma}^2_{(i=0)}$, $f'_{r2_{min}}(x_{0min})$ is minimum for $\lambda_m = \lambda_{max}$ (with λ_{max} the maximum eigenvalue of $\mathbf{R}_H$) and maximum for $\lambda_m = 0$. We can then minimize $\hat{\sigma}^2_{(i=0)}$:

$$\frac{8}{27} \frac{(\lambda_{max} + \sigma^2 + \hat{\sigma}^2_{(i=0)})^2}{(\lambda_{max} + \sigma^2)^2} \geq 1$$

$$\Leftrightarrow \hat{\sigma}^2_{(i=0)} \geq (\sqrt{\frac{27}{8}} - 1)(\lambda_{max} + \sigma^2). \qquad [2.49]$$

The necessary condition $\max_x(f'_2(x)) > 1$ is reached for $\hat{\sigma}^2_{(i=0)} \geq (\sqrt{\frac{27}{8}} - 1)(\lambda_{max} + \sigma^2)$. Since λ_{max} and σ^2 are unknown, the condition is necessary but not sufficient so as to assess that f_2 has a fixed point that is different from zero. However, λ_{max} is, by definition, the maximum eigenvalue of the channel covariance matrix; therefore, $\lambda_{max} \geq \frac{1}{M} \sum_{m=0}^{M-1} \lambda_m$. Furthermore, as $M_2 = \frac{1}{M} \sum_{m=0}^{M-1} \lambda_m + \sigma^2$, so, due to [2.49] we can minimize $\hat{\sigma}^2_{(i=0)}$, and get

$$\hat{\sigma}^2_{(i=0)} \geq (\sqrt{\frac{27}{8}} - 1)M_2. \qquad [2.50]$$

2.2.2.3. *Sufficient condition for the convergence of the sequence* $(\hat{\sigma}^2_{(i)})$

The lower bound [2.50] satisfies the necessary condition $f'_{r2} \geq 1$. Thus, this entails that f_{r2} has a fixed point that is different from zero. In order to give a sufficient condition, the initialization value $\hat{\sigma}^2_{(i=0)}$ has to be set equal to ΛM_2, with $\Lambda \gg 1$. Indeed, for all $x \in [0, M_2]$, f_{r2} satisfies

$$\lim_{\hat{\sigma}^2_{(i=0)} \to +\infty} f_{r2}(x) = M_2. \qquad [2.51]$$

Therefore, it is possible to find $\hat{\sigma}^2_{(i=0)}$ such that $f_{r2}(x) > x$. Given that $\lim_{x \to +\infty} f_{r2}(x) = M_2$, we deduce that a fixed point different from zero exists for a well-chosen initialization $\hat{\sigma}^2_{(i=0)} = \Lambda M_2$. However, the previous development only proves the existence of a sufficient condition on $\hat{\sigma}^2_{(i=0)}$ for the convergence of $(\hat{\sigma}^2_{(i)})$ to a non-null limit, but it does not give a precise characterization of $\hat{\sigma}^2_{(i=0)}$. In order to get a suitable value of $\hat{\sigma}^2_{(i=0)}$, the receiver should test some initialization values (e.g. due to an abacus) until it finds the expected one, as shown in Figure 2.12. It illustrates the shape of f_{r2} considering $\sigma^2 = 2$ for two examples: one with a relevant initialization $\hat{\sigma}^2_{(i=0)} = 10M_2$ (we see a fixed point that is different from zero) and the other with an initialization which does not match the necessary condition (zero is the sole fixed point). It is then verified that if $\hat{\sigma}^2_{(i=0)}$ is not chosen large enough, then $\hat{\sigma}^2_{(i)}$ converges to zero. A second drawback arises: the ratio between the noise variance σ^2 to be estimated and the initialization $\hat{\sigma}^2_{(i=0)}$ is not constant for all values of σ^2, as shown in Figure 2.13 for $\Lambda = 10$ and $P_s = 1$. Indeed, Figure 2.13 depicts the noise variance σ^2 and its estimation $\hat{\sigma}^2$ versus σ^2. Thus, a given value Λ can be well chosen for a given value σ^2 but not for another one. The solution is then not appropriate if the noise variance has a varying level during the transmission.

In order to get the optimal value $\sigma^2_{(i=0)}$, an abacus with different curves of f_{r2} can be created. However, the solution is not applicable in practice, since the channel frequency response and the noise variance can take an infinite number of values. Furthermore, we assume that the receiver has no *a priori* knowledge of the set of parameters $\{\lambda_m, \sigma^2\}$, which makes the *a priori* choice of the optimal initialization impossible. A solution close to the optimal one is nevertheless proposed in the next section.

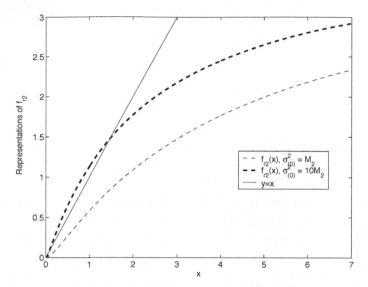

Figure 2.12. *Shape of f_{r2} in two different cases, compared with $y = x$*

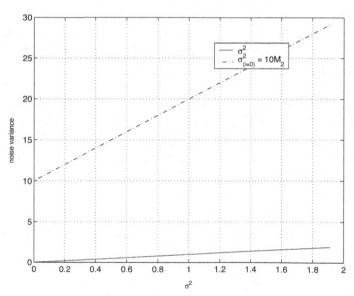

Figure 2.13. σ^2 *and* $\hat{\sigma}^2_{(i=0)}$ *versus* σ^2

2.2.2.4. *Optimal choice of the initialization* $\hat{\sigma}^2_{(i=0)}$

The conditions on $\hat{\sigma}^2_{(i=0)}$ given in the previous sections are either not relevant enough ($\hat{\sigma}^2_{(i=0)} = \Lambda M_2$ with $\Lambda \gg 1$) or too complex (use of abacus of f_2). Here, a simple characterization of $\hat{\sigma}^2_{(i=0)}$ is proposed due to the noise variance estimation $\hat{\sigma}^2$, which is performed on the last frame. It supposes that the noise variance does not vary significantly from one frame to another. If we denote by n_F the index of the current frame, the proposed method is:

– For the first frame $n_F = 1$, perform the algorithm due to the arbitrary initialization $\hat{\sigma}^2_{(i=0)} = \Lambda M_2$ chosen with the sufficient condition $\Lambda \gg 1$.

– For $n_F > 1$, get the noise variance $\hat{\sigma}^2$ and the eigenvalues of the channel covariance matrix $\tilde{\underline{\mathbf{R}}}_H^{LMMSE}$ [2.33], estimated at the previous frame $n_F - 1$.

– Considering the expression of f_{r2} given in [2.43], look for $\hat{\sigma}^2_{(i=0),opt}$ so that

$$\frac{\hat{\sigma}^4}{M} \sum_{m=0}^{M-1} \frac{\lambda_m + \hat{\sigma}^2}{\left(\frac{(\lambda_m + \hat{\sigma}^2)^3}{(\lambda_m + \hat{\sigma}^2 + \hat{\sigma}^2_{(i=0),opt})^2} + \hat{\sigma}^2 \right)^2} - \hat{\sigma}^2 = 0. \qquad [2.52]$$

The direct solution of [2.52] is very complex, but in practice, the receiver can use a simple binary search algorithm to approach the optimal solution. This solution $\hat{\sigma}^2_{(i=0),opt}$, close to the optimal one, can then be found at the frame n_F by means of the previous estimation. The next section analyzes the performance of the proposed algorithm and finally shows that the performance in the realistic scenario is close to the performance of the theoretical case.

2.2.3. *Simulations results: realistic approach*

The parameters used for the simulations are exactly the same as the ones used for the theoretical scenario.

2.2.3.1. *Convergence of the noise variance estimation*

Similar to Figure 2.6, Figure 2.14 shows the noise variance estimation versus the iteration number, from $i = 0$ to $i = 20$. In order to validate the results for all SNR values, two values are considered: $\rho = 0$ dB and $\rho = 10$ dB. The initialization is chosen according to the sufficient condition $\sigma^2_{(i=0)} = 20M_2$. The curves of the practical case are compared to that of the theoretical scenario (with $\mathbf{R}_H$) and the exact value σ^2. The curves are obtained after 4,000 simulation runs.

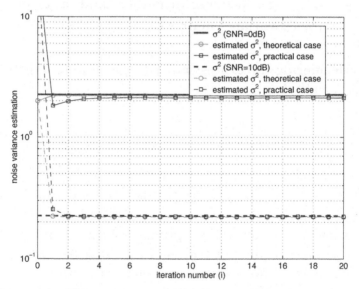

Figure 2.14. *Noise variance estimation versus the iteration number, comparison to the theoretical case. For a color version of the figure, see www.iste.co.uk/savaux/mmse.zip*

For iterations $i \geq 1$, Figure 2.14 shows that the sequence $(\hat{\sigma}^2_{(i)})$ is monotonous and converges to a sole non-null value, which verifies the theoretical developments given in section 2.2.2. Even in the practical case, the algorithm quickly converges, since from $i = 7$, the noise variance estimation seems to reach its limit. This observation will be confirmed in the next section. Figure 2.14 also characterizes the noise variance estimation due to the normalized bias β calculated by $\beta = |(\hat{\sigma}^2_{(i)}) - \sigma^2|/\sigma^2$. Expressed in percentage, the bias of the proposed estimation is equal to 5.9% for $\rho = 0$ dB and 1.2% for $\rho = 10$ dB. These results are very close to the estimation performed in the perfect case. It also shows that the method is less accurate for low SNR values, which can be explained by the fact that the ratio between σ^2 and $\hat{\sigma}^2_{(i=0)}$ is not constant according to the level of the noise variance.

2.2.3.2. *Characterization of the threshold e_σ*

Figure 2.15 depicts the values of the difference $|\hat{\sigma}^2_{(i)} - \hat{\sigma}^2_{(i-1)}|$ versus the number of iterations for $i \geq 2$. The practical case is compared with the theoretical case performed with $\underline{\mathbf{R}}_H$. Simulations are performed with $\rho = 10$ dB and the initialization value $\hat{\sigma}^2_{(i=0)} = 2$ in the theoretical case and $\hat{\sigma}^2_{(i=0)} = 20M_2$ in the practical case. These curves evaluate the required number of iterations to get an expected value of the threshold e_σ.

Although the gradient of $|\hat{\sigma}^2_{(i)} - \hat{\sigma}^2_{(i-1)}|$ is smaller in the practical case than it is in the theoretical case, Figure 2.15 confirms that $|\hat{\sigma}^2_{(i)} - \hat{\sigma}^2_{(i-1)}|$ converges to zero. It also allows us to evaluate the required number of iterations, considering a given threshold value. For instance, in order to reach $e_\sigma = 0.01$, three iterations are required in the practical case and two in the perfect case. For $e_\sigma = 0.0001$, seven iterations are required in the practical case and three in the perfect case.

2.2.3.3. *Comparison of SNR estimation with other methods*

Figure 2.16 depicts the NMSE of the SNR estimation of the proposed method for the practical scenario, and compares it to Ren's method [REN 09], Xu's method [XU 05b] and the usual M_2M_4 method [XU 05a]. We recall that Ren's method requires a two pilot symbols preamble in order to avoid the effect of the frequency selective channel, whereas Xu's method and the M_2M_4 method require only one pilot symbol. Figures 2.16(a) and (b) compare the SNR estimation performed with two different initializations. For Figure 2.16(a), the sufficient condition $\hat{\sigma}^2_{(i=0)} = 20M_2$ is considered at each frame. In Figure 2.16(b), the initialization step $\hat{\sigma}^2_{(i=0)} = 20M_2$ is used for the first frame $n_{\mathcal{F}} = 1$, and then $\hat{\sigma}^2_{(i=0)}$ is updated due to the proposed method presented in section 2.2.2.4. Whether Figure 2.16(a) or (b) is considered, the number of iterations i_f is set to 7. In the theoretical case, the initialization value is $\hat{\sigma}^2_{(i=0)} = 0.1$ and the number of iterations is $i_f = 3$. The NMSE given by $NMSE = E\{|\hat{\rho} - \rho|^2/\rho^2\}$ is approximated and simulated due to an average made over 200,000 samples.

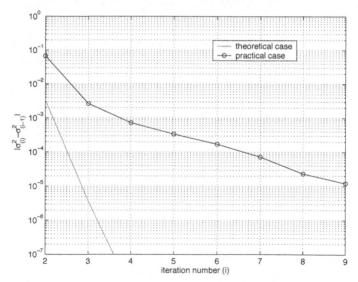

Figure 2.15. $|\hat{\sigma}^2_{(i)} - \hat{\sigma}^2_{(i-1)}|$ *versus the iteration number* i

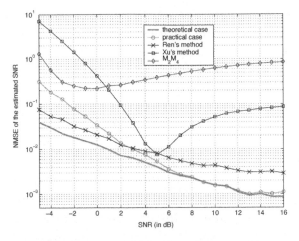

a) Sufficient initialization $\sigma^2_{(i=0)} = 20M_2$

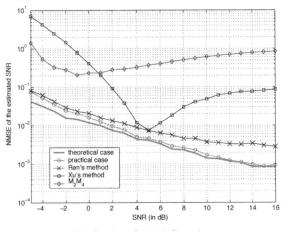

b) Optimal initialization

Figure 2.16. *NMSE of the SNR estimation of the proposed method compared to three existing methods for two different initializations. For a color version of the figure, see www.iste.co.uk/savaux/mmse.zip*

As previously mentioned for the theoretical scenario and noticed in [XU 05a], the performance of the M_2M_4 method is degraded in Rayleigh channels. Unlike the theoretical case performed with $\breve{\mathbf{R}}_H$, the proposed iterative method outperforms the Xu's method, whatever the considered SNR. In Figure 2.16(a), the performance of the algorithm is degraded compared to the one obtained using Ren's method for low SNR values (<3 dB). It confirms the observations made concerning the evaluation of the bias, that is for low values of SNR, $\hat{\sigma}^2_{(i=0)}$ is not large enough compared to the value of the noise variance σ^2. However, when the algorithm is used with an updated initialization (Figure 2.16(b)), the method outperforms the Ren's method for all SNR values is, and the SNR gap with the perfect case is less than 1 dB from $SNR = 0$ dB. This proves the efficiency of the proposed algorithm and the validity of the improvement with regard to the choice of $\hat{\sigma}^2_{(i=0)}$, when performed with an update on each frame. Compared to the other methods, the proposed algorithm improves the trade-off between the number of required pilots and the performance of the SNR estimation.

2.2.3.4. *Channel estimation*

Figure 2.17 shows the BER curves of the proposed estimator versus the SNR and for $i = 1, 2, 4$ and $i = 7$. It also compares the results with the theoretical scenario, the perfect estimation and the usual LS. The simulation parameters are exactly the same as the ones used to simulate Figure 2.10. The BER curves are obtained by averaging the errors over a stream of 2.5×10^6 bits.

We observe that the proposed method converges after few iterations, and outperforms again the LS estimator. Furthermore, after seven iterations of the algorithm, the gap between the BER curve of the proposed method and the perfect estimation is less than 0.2 dB. The iterative estimation performed in the practical scenario almost reaches the performance of the theoretical one.

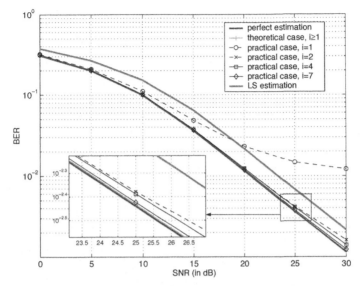

Figure 2.17. *Bit error rate (BER) of the proposed method versus SNR, and comparison with perfect estimation, theoretical case and LS. For a color version of the figure, see www.iste.co.uk/savaux/mmse.zip*

2.3. Summary

In this chapter, we have presented an algorithm for the joint estimation of the noise variance and the channel. Its goal is to reach the optimal MMSE estimation while avoiding the necessity of *a priori* knowing the second-order moments of the noise and the channel. To this end, each estimator (noise and channel) iteratively feeds the other one in order to return a couple of estimated values $(\hat{\mathbf{H}}_{i_f}, \hat{\sigma}^2_{i_f})$. The method has been first developed in a theoretical case and then extended to a more realistic scenario in which the channel covariance is unknown and has to be estimated. It has been proved that the algorithm converges according to an appropriate initialization value, and simulations have shown the accuracy of both estimations. In addition to the joint estimation technique, we will show in the next chapter that the algorithm can also be used as a spectrum sensing algorithm.

3

Application of the Algorithm as a Detector for Cognitive Radio Systems

In the previous chapter, the algorithm was presented when an OFDM signal is presented in a given band, such that the joint estimation is performed on a pilot preamble. This chapter aims to show the ability of the proposed algorithm (in the practical scenario) to be used as a free band detector. First, a brief state of the art of spectrum sensing techniques is provided. Second, it will be shown that the algorithm converges even when it is fed by noise only, hence it is proposed to use the estimator as a signal detector. In the third part, an analysis of the detection and false alarm probabilities are presented, and then simulations show the performance of the method.

3.1. Spectrum sensing

The multiplication of the applications and services in wireless communications leads to a constant increase of data rate-consuming transmissions, while the usable spectrum is naturally limited and most of the bands are already allocated to specific licenses. Dynamic spectrum access is then an attractive solution to use the spectrum resource at its full capacity, as far as some of these licensed bands are not used at full capacity [SPE 02], so that white spaces are useable in the time–frequency plan. To this end, away from the usual paradigm in which the channels are allocated only for licensed users, Joseph Mitola defined the cognitive radio [MIT 99] enabling an opportunistic access by unlicensed users to the unused frequency bands. In such a network, the opportunistic users, called secondary users (SUs) can use licensed bands when primary users (PUs) are absent from those bands, as depicted in Figure 3.1 where the colorful squares depict the PUs' signals and the white squares are the free bands. The mandatory condition for the SUs to use the licensed bands is to minimize the interferences with PUs. Thus, they must be able to sense the presence of the PUs, even if the PU's signal is attenuated compared to the noise level.

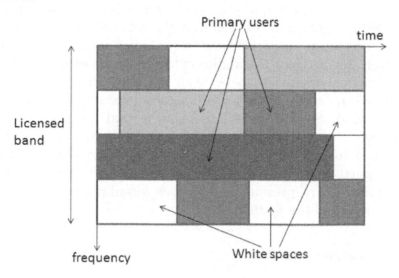

Figure 3.1. *White spaces in a licensed band enabling an opportunistic access for SUs. For a color version of the figure, see www.iste.co.uk / savaux / mmse.zip*

The process set up by the SUs to sense the presence of the PUs is called spectrum sensing. The authors of [YÜC 09, LU 12, AXE 12] propose detailed reviews of the different techniques of spectrum sensing of the literature. The different methods are usually classified into two main categories: the non-cooperative detection and the cooperative detection.

3.1.1. *Non-cooperative methods*

The non-cooperative detection regards a sole SU who tries to detect the presence of the PU without sharing information with other SUs. Among the wide range of methods [YÜC 09, LU 12, AXE 12, KHA 13], we can briefly describe the main ones.

The energy detector (ED) or radiometer is the simplest technique since it just measures the energy of the received signal and compares it to a threshold. Its low complexity of implementation and independence from the PU's signal features make the ED a frequently used detector. However, the choice of the threshold value depends on the noise variance, and uncertainties on the noise level may cause important degradations of the detector performance [TAN 08, JOU 11].

When the PU's signal is supposed to be known at the receiver, the matched-filter detector calculates the correlation between the known signal and the received signal and compares the peaks in the correlation function to a threshold [PRO 08, PRI 61]. This is the optimal detector when the signal is transmitted over an additive white Gaussian noise (AWGN) channel, but due to the strong hypotheses on the knowledge of the PU's signal, this method is generally not applicable in practice, and its performance is degraded when the knowledge of the signal is erroneous [SAH 04].

Less binding than the matched-filter, the feature detectors only use several characteristics of the signal to detect the PU. Thus, the waveform-based sensing uses the preamble of the

PU's signal (used for the synchronization, the estimation etc.) to perform a correlation with the received signal [TAN 05]. However, the performance of the waveform-based sensing is degraded in the presence of selective channels. More generally, the cyclostationarity detector exploits the periodic redundancy of all human-made telecommunications signals to differentiate them from a pure Gaussian noise [GAR 91, LUN 07, KHA 14]. As indicated in [AXE 12], the redundancy can be due to periodic patterns such as the cyclic prefix (CP) (the peaks in the autocorrelation function appear at time-lag T_s), the symbol rate or the channel coding. However, these second-order detectors require large sensing time, i.e. a large number of symbols to reach a sufficient statistics. In [KHA 10], a hybrid architecture composed of both energy and cyclostationarity is proposed. It allows us to compensate the limitation of the ED due to the noise uncertainty due to a cyclostationarity detection stage whose computation time is reduced.

Another attractive technique called eigenvalue-based detection uses the characteristics of the signal covariance matrix of large-sized random matrices (i.e. when filled with noise samples) as presented in [CAR 08, ZEN 09, PEN 09]. The large-sized matrices require a great number of sensors and a long sensing time. If this condition is fulfilled, the random matrix theory would prove that the distribution of the eigenvalues of such matrix tends to a deterministic function. Two main techniques are proposed in the literature for the signal detection using this distribution: in [CAR 08], if the noise variance is known, the signal is detected if a peak appears outside of the domain of the function. Using the same theory, the authors of [ZEN 09] propose the maximum–minimum eigenvalue (MME) detection, whose principle consists of comparing the ratio between the maximum and minimum eigenvalues with a threshold to take the decision. Based on the same theory, both techniques have the same asymptotic performance, but the latter does not require the noise level to be performed. However, these two methods require matrices with very large sizes, which means a large number of sensors and a long sensing time. In order to use MME detection with a single sensor, the authors of [LIU 13] propose to artificially create a large matrix by stacking the shifted vectors of the received sampled signal. However, this method is limited due to the correlation between the rows of the created matrix.

3.1.2. Cooperative methods

In the cooperative detection scenario, several SUs (called nodes of the network) share some information about the state of the spectrum. This sharing allows the SUs to increase the probability of detection of the PU, in particular for the SUs who might receive the PU's signal disrupted by fading or noise uncertainty, and it also allows us to reduce the sensing time. However, this information sharing requires a delay and uses bandwidth, which is a challenge in cooperative detection. The different cooperative techniques can be summed up as follows.

When each SU transmits its sensing data to a central unit called fusion center, we say that the detection is made with soft combing (or centralized) decision. The fusion center then combines the different soft decisions to make a decision in the presence or the absence of the PU, and this decision is transmitted back to the SUs. In [MA 07], the performance of different data combination schemes are compared. Although it is considered as the optimal detection scheme, the required bandwidth to transmit the sensing information from the SUs and the computation complexity of the data processing might be large, according to the sensing method.

In the detection with hard combining (or distributed) decision, each SU makes its own decision and transmits to the fusion center a binary information 0 or 1. The fusion center then combines the hard decisions of the SUs to make a common decision. The decision can be made by following the AND-logic, the OR-logic or the voting rule [AXE 12, KHA 13]. Although the hard decision is less efficient than the soft decision, it is also less complex and less bandwidth consuming. Furthermore, if a large number of nodes is considered, the hard decision and the soft decision become equivalent in terms of performance [KHA 13].

The fully distributed detection differs from the previous detection in the sense that no fusion center is considered in the network. However, both approaches are often mistaken in the literature and are simply called "distributed detection". In [IUT 13], an example of fully distributed detection algorithm is given: at each iteration, a sensing step followed by a gossiping step is performed. In the gossiping step, the SUs transmit the results of the sensing step to their neighbors, without the help of a fusion center. This approach appears as efficient in the case of an SU who is hidden from the PU by an obstacle.

For the external detection, the sensing process is not performed by the SUs, but by external sensors. According to the arrangement of the sensors in the networks, the external detection also avoids the hidden SUs effect. As mentioned in [KHA 13], this solution is developed in the IEEE 802.22 standard, designed for the opportunistic access to the free TV bands.

In addition to these two main differences, the detection techniques can also be differentiated according to the bandwidth on which they are performed. Indeed, some methods can detect several holes over a wide bandwidth, while others are adapted to the detection of a sole hole in a given channel. Since the proposed algorithms are performed by a sole receiver in a given channel, its application to spectrum sensing will be classified in the non-cooperative technique. More precisely, since it uses the MMSE criterion, this is a second-order moment based detector.

3.2. Proposed detector

3.2.1. *Detection hypothesis*

Let us consider the problem of the detection by an SU of a preamble in an PU's OFDM signal over a Rayleigh channel in a given band to be sensed. The SU has no *a priori* knowledge of the presence or the absence of the PU, so the detection hypothesis test is written as follows:

$$\begin{cases} \mathbb{H}_0 & : \mathbf{U} = \mathbf{W} \\ \mathbb{H}_1 & : \mathbf{U} = \underline{\mathbf{C}}\mathbf{H} + \mathbf{W}, \end{cases} \qquad [3.1]$$

where $\mathbb{H}_0$ and $\mathbb{H}_1$ denote the absence and the presence of the PU hypotheses, respectively. Note that the matrix $\underline{\mathbf{C}}$ corresponds to a preamble, such as $\mathbb{H}_1$ corresponds to the model developed in the previous chapter. Furthermore, the hypothesis test in [3.1] is written assuming a perfect synchronization. As the SU does not have any knowledge about the presence or the absence of the signal, it is more realistic to consider a synchronization mismatch as in [1.18]. Consequently, the test [3.1] is rewritten as:

$$\begin{cases} \mathbb{H}_0 & : \mathbf{U} = \mathbf{W} \\ \mathbb{H}_1 & : \mathbf{U} = \underline{\mathbf{C}}\mathbf{H} + \mathbf{I}(\delta) + \mathbf{W}. \end{cases} \qquad [3.2]$$

The performance of a detector is characterized by its probability of detection, denoted as P_d, and its false alarm probability P_{fa}. P_d corresponds to the probability of choosing the correct $\mathbb{H}_1$ while the signal is present, whereas P_{fa} corresponds to the probability of choosing $\mathbb{H}_1$ while the signal is absent. In a general way, the closer P_d is to 1 and P_{fa} to 0, the more the detector is efficient. It is also usual to use the missing probability $P_m = 1 - P_d$, as the probability of choosing $\mathbb{H}_0$ while the signal is present.

As mentioned in [KHA 13, IUT 13], the sensibility of the detector (the expected value of P_{fa} and P_d) depends on the application. In a cognitive radio context, the SU has to minimize the interference with the PU, so the probability of detection has to be maximized, whereas if the false alarm probability is not optimized, it only implies that the SU misses white spaces. However, in a radar application, a false alarm could have serious consequences, especially in a military context.

In the previous chapter, the convergence of the algorithm under $\mathbb{H}_1$ has been shown. In the following sections, the convergence of the algorithm under $\mathbb{H}_0$ is studied, and an analytical expression of P_d and P_{fa} is also proposed.

3.2.2. Convergence of the MMSE-based algorithm under the hypothesis $\mathbb{H}_0$

The signal $\underline{\mathbf{C}}$ is now supposed to be absent, so the received signal is written as $\mathbf{U} = \mathbf{W}$. The convergence of the proposed algorithm in the absence of signal is going to be proved. Furthermore, it will be shown later that the convergence to a non-null solution enables the MMSE-based algorithm to be a free band detector. To this end, the first three steps of algorithm 2 presented in section 2.2 are now expressed under the hypothesis $\mathbb{H}_0$.

3.2.2.1. *Expression of the algorithm under* $\mathbb{H}_0$

Let us consider that the receiver does not know if the signal is present or absent, so the same formalism as in section 2.2 is used, and the steps of the algorithm are recalled:

1) First, the LS channel estimation is performed:

$$\hat{\mathbf{H}}^{LS} = \underline{\mathbf{C}}^{-1}\mathbf{U} = \underline{\mathbf{C}}^{-1}\mathbf{W}. \tag{3.3}$$

The channel covariance matrix

$$\tilde{\underline{\mathbf{R}}}_H^{LS} = \hat{\mathbf{H}}^{LS}(\hat{\mathbf{H}}^{LS})^H = \mathbf{W}\mathbf{W}^H \tag{3.4}$$

is deduced from [3.3]. Furthermore, a stopping criterion e_σ and an initialization $\hat{\sigma}^2_{(i=0)}$ are set.

2) At iteration $i = 1$ of the algorithm, the LMMSE channel estimation $\hat{\mathbf{H}}^{LMMSE}_{(i=1)}$ is performed by using $\tilde{\underline{\mathbf{R}}}^{LS}_H$:

$$\hat{\mathbf{H}}^{LMMSE}_{(i=1)} = \tilde{\underline{\mathbf{R}}}^{LS}_H (\tilde{\underline{\mathbf{R}}}^{LS}_H + \hat{\sigma}^2_{(i=0)}\underline{\mathbf{I}})^{-1}\hat{\mathbf{H}}^{LS}. \qquad [3.5]$$

3) The MMSE noise variance estimation $\hat{\sigma}^2_{(i=1)}$ is performed with $\hat{\mathbf{H}} = \hat{\mathbf{H}}^{LMMSE}_{(i=1)}$:

$$\hat{\sigma}^2_{(i=1)} = \frac{1}{M}E\{||\hat{\mathbf{H}}^{LS} - \hat{\mathbf{H}}^{LMMSE}_{(i=1)}||^2_F\}, \qquad [3.6]$$

and a new covariance matrix is computed by:

$$\tilde{\underline{\mathbf{R}}}^{LMMSE}_H = \hat{\mathbf{H}}^{LMMSE}_{(i=1)} (\hat{\mathbf{H}}^{LMMSE}_{(i=1)})^H. \qquad [3.7]$$

Indeed, it is proved in Appendix 2 that if the algorithm keeps on computing with $\tilde{\mathbf{R}}^{LS}_H = \mathbf{W}\mathbf{W}^H$, then the sequence $\hat{\sigma}^2_{(i)}$ necessarily converges to zero. When $\tilde{\underline{\mathbf{R}}}^{LS}_H$ is used, in spite of its inputs being different, the algorithm has exactly the same response whether hypothesis $\mathbb{H}_0$ or $\mathbb{H}_1$.

Then, for $i \geq 2$, perform the channel and the noise variance estimation:

$$\hat{\mathbf{H}}^{LMMSE}_{(i)} = \tilde{\underline{\mathbf{R}}}^{LMMSE}_H (\tilde{\underline{\mathbf{R}}}^{LMMSE}_H + \hat{\sigma}^2_{(i-1)}\underline{\mathbf{I}})^{-1}\hat{\mathbf{H}}^{LS}, \qquad [3.8]$$

$$\hat{\sigma}^2_{(i)} = \frac{1}{M}E\{||\hat{\mathbf{H}}^{LS} - \hat{\mathbf{H}}^{LMMSE}_{(i)}||^2\}. \qquad [3.9]$$

For the application of the algorithm to spectrum sensing, it only requires these three steps.

3.2.2.2. Scalar expression of the sequence $(\hat{\sigma}^2_{(i)})$

As it has been done under $\mathbb{H}_1$ in section 2.2, we first get a scalar expression from [3.7], and the convergence of the extracted sequence is proved. Recalling that $\tilde{\underline{\mathbf{R}}}_H^{LS}$ is an Hermitian matrix, we develop [3.7] as:

$$
\begin{aligned}
\tilde{\underline{\mathbf{R}}}_H^{LMMSE} &= \hat{\mathbf{H}}_{(i=1)}^{LMMSE}(\hat{\mathbf{H}}_{(i=1)}^{LMMSE})^H \\
&= \tilde{\underline{\mathbf{R}}}_H^{LS}(\tilde{\underline{\mathbf{R}}}_H^{LS} + \hat{\sigma}_{(i=0)}^2\underline{\mathbf{I}})^{-1}\hat{\mathbf{H}}^{LS}(\tilde{\underline{\mathbf{R}}}_H^{LS} \\
&\quad \times (\tilde{\underline{\mathbf{R}}}_H^{LS} + \hat{\sigma}_{(i=0)}^2\underline{\mathbf{I}})^{-1}\hat{\mathbf{H}}^{LS})^H \\
&= \tilde{\underline{\mathbf{R}}}_H^{LS}(\tilde{\underline{\mathbf{R}}}_H^{LS} + \hat{\sigma}_{(i=0)}^2\underline{\mathbf{I}})^{-1}\hat{\mathbf{H}}^{LS}(\hat{\mathbf{H}}^{LS})^H \\
&\quad \times (\tilde{\underline{\mathbf{R}}}_H^{LS}(\tilde{\underline{\mathbf{R}}}_H^{LS} + \hat{\sigma}_{(i=0)}^2\underline{\mathbf{I}})^{-1}). \quad\quad [3.10]
\end{aligned}
$$

Let us assume that M is large enough to justify the approximation $tr(\mathbf{W}\mathbf{W}^H) = tr(\sigma^2\mathbf{I})$. Since the estimation of the noise variance is calculated by means of the trace in [3.9], we make the assumption that, as a first approximation $\tilde{\underline{\mathbf{R}}}_H^{LS} \approx \sigma^2\mathbf{I}$, then it possible to replace $\mathbf{R}_H^{LMMSE}$ by:

$$
\begin{aligned}
\tilde{\underline{\mathbf{R}}}_H^{LMMSE} &= \sigma^2\underline{\mathbf{I}}(\sigma^2\underline{\mathbf{I}} + \hat{\sigma}_{(i=0)}^2\underline{\mathbf{I}})^{-1}\tilde{\underline{\mathbf{R}}}_H^{LS}(\sigma^2\underline{\mathbf{I}}(\sigma^2\underline{\mathbf{I}} + \hat{\sigma}_{(i=0)}^2\underline{\mathbf{I}})^{-1}) \\
&= \frac{\sigma^6}{(\sigma^2 + \hat{\sigma}_{(i=0)}^2)^2}\underline{\mathbf{I}} \quad\quad\quad [3.11]
\end{aligned}
$$

in [3.9]. Thus, by reinjecting [3.11] in [3.8] and [3.9], it yields:

$$
\begin{aligned}
\hat{\sigma}_{(i+1)}^2 &= \frac{1}{M}E\{\|\hat{\mathbf{H}}^{LS} - \hat{\mathbf{H}}_{(i+1)}^{LMMSE}\|^2\} \\
&= \frac{1}{M}E\{\|\hat{\mathbf{H}}^{LS} - \tilde{\underline{\mathbf{R}}}_H^{LMMSE}(\tilde{\underline{\mathbf{R}}}_H^{LMMSE} + \hat{\sigma}_{(i)}^2\underline{\mathbf{I}})^{-1}\hat{\mathbf{H}}^{LS}\|^2\} \\
&= \frac{1}{M}E\left\{\|\mathbf{W} - \frac{\sigma^6}{(\sigma^2 + \hat{\sigma}_{(i=0)}^2)^2}\underline{\mathbf{I}}(\frac{\sigma^6}{(\sigma^2 + \hat{\sigma}_{(i=0)}^2)^2}\underline{\mathbf{I}} \right. \\
&\quad \left. + \hat{\sigma}_{(i)}^2\underline{\mathbf{I}})^{-1}\mathbf{W}\|^2\right\}
\end{aligned}
$$

$$= \frac{1}{M} E \left\{ ||(\hat{\sigma}^2_{(i)}\underline{\mathbf{I}}((\frac{\sigma^6}{(\sigma^2 + \hat{\sigma}^2_{(i=0)})^2} + \hat{\sigma}^2_{(i)})\underline{\mathbf{I}})^{-1})\mathbf{W}||^2 \right\}$$

$$= \frac{\sigma^2 \hat{\sigma}^4_{(i)}(\sigma^2 + \hat{\sigma}^2_{(i=0)})^4}{(\sigma^6 + \hat{\sigma}^2_{(i)}(\sigma^2 + \hat{\sigma}^2_{(i=0)})^2)^2}. \qquad [3.12]$$

3.2.2.3. Convergence of the sequence $(\hat{\sigma}^2_{(i)})$ to a non-null solution

For a better readability, we note in the following mathematical developments:

$$A = \sigma^2 + \hat{\sigma}^2_{(i=0)}. \qquad [3.13]$$

It is once again noticeable that the sequence $(\hat{\sigma}^2_{(i+1)})$ is built from a function f_{s1} such as, if we note $x = \hat{\sigma}^2_{(i)}$:

$$f_{s1}(x) = \frac{\sigma^2 A^4 x^2}{(\sigma^6 + A^2 x)^2}. \qquad [3.14]$$

The sequence converges if f_{s1} has at least one fixed point. Zero is an obvious fixed point, but it has been proved in Appendix 2 that the algorithm enters into an endless loop if $(\hat{\sigma}^2_{(i)})$ converges to zero. We then solve the equation $f_{s1}(x) = x$ to find the others fixed points:

$$f_{s1}(x) = x$$
$$\Leftrightarrow \frac{\sigma^2 A^4 x^2}{(\sigma^6 + A^2 x)^2} = x$$
$$\Leftrightarrow \sigma^2 A^4 x^2 = x(\sigma^6 + A^2 x)^2. \qquad [3.15]$$

Since we consider that zero is not a solution to the equation, the previous expressions can be simplified by x, and the problem amounts to look for real roots of the polynomial $A^4 x^2 + x(2A^2\sigma^6 - \sigma^2 A^4) + \sigma^{12}$. Since it is a second order polynomial whose real solutions are looked for, the first condition on the initialization $\hat{\sigma}^2_{(i=0)}$ is to obtain a positive discriminant $\Delta = (2A^2\sigma^6 - \sigma^2 A^4)^2 - 4A^4\sigma^{12}$, i.e.:

$$\Delta \geq 0$$

$$\Leftrightarrow (2A^2\sigma^6 - \sigma^2 A^4)^2 \geq 4A^4\sigma^{12}$$

$$\Leftrightarrow \hat{\sigma}^2_{(i=0)} \geq 3\sigma^2. \qquad [3.16]$$

As σ^2 is absolutely unknown, we can find a stronger condition on $\hat{\sigma}^2_{(i=0)}$, conditionally to $\Delta > 0$. We then find the roots r_s^+ and r_{s-} of the polynomial under the condition $\Delta > 0$:

$$r_{s-}^+ = \frac{(\sigma^2 A^4 - 2A^2\sigma^6)^+_- \sqrt{(2A^2\sigma^6 - \sigma^2 A^4)^2 - 4A^4\sigma^{12}}}{2A^4}$$

$$\Leftrightarrow r_{s-}^+ = \frac{(\sigma^2 A^2 - 2\sigma^6)^+_- \sqrt{\sigma^4 A^4 - 4\sigma^8 A^2}}{2A^2}. \qquad [3.17]$$

Note that when $\hat{\sigma}^2_{(i=0)}$ tends to $+\infty$, then $A = \sigma^2 + \hat{\sigma}^2_{(i=0)}$ also tends to $+\infty$, hence:

$$\lim_{A \to \infty} r_s^+ = \frac{\sigma^2 A^2 + \sigma^2 A^2}{2A^2} = \sigma^2, \qquad [3.18]$$

and

$$\lim_{A \to \infty} r_{s-} = \frac{\sigma^2 A^2 - \sigma^2 A^2}{2A^2} = 0. \qquad [3.19]$$

It can be seen that, by choosing the initialization value $\hat{\sigma}^2_{(i=0)}$ as large as wanted, the sequence $(\hat{\sigma}^2_{(i)})$ converges to a value as close as possible to the exact value of the noise variance σ^2. This characterization of the initialization value $\hat{\sigma}^2_{(i=0)}$ perfectly matches the one made for the sufficient condition under hypothesis $\mathbb{H}_1$ in section 2.2.2.3. Furthermore, it will be shown that this solution allows the receiver to detect the PU in the tested band. Thus, choosing

$\hat{\sigma}^2_{(i=0)}$ with a large value is the condition for the algorithm to converge to a non-null solution for both hypotheses $\mathbb{H}_0$ and $\mathbb{H}_1$. Furthermore, since it converges, the stopping criterion $|\hat{\sigma}^2_{(i)} - \hat{\sigma}^2_{(i-1)}| < e_\sigma$ can also be the same under $\mathbb{H}_0$. Finally, the MMSE-based algorithm can be used as a free band detector.

Figure 3.2 displays the function f_{s1} for different values of $(\hat{\sigma}^2_{(i=0)})$, compared to $y = x$ and a fixed $\sigma^2 = 1$. By comparing the curves of f_{s1} for different initializations values, we verify that, the larger the value of $\hat{\sigma}^2_{(i=0)}$, the closer the fixed point to the real value of $\sigma^2 = 1$.

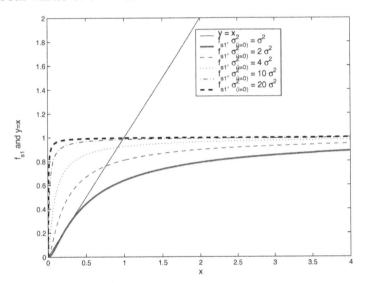

Figure 3.2. *Shape of f_{s1} for different initialization values $\sigma^2_{(i=0)}$ for $\sigma^2 = 1$ and compared to $y = x$. For a color version of the figure, see www.iste.co.uk/savaux/mmse.zip*

3.2.3. *Decision rule for the proposed detector*

In this section, a decision rule for the detector is proposed. To this end, whatever $\mathbb{H}_0$ or $\mathbb{H}_1$, it is supposed that the algorithm has converged, i.e. the condition $|\hat{\sigma}^2_{(i)} - \hat{\sigma}^2_{(i-1)}| < e_\sigma$ is reached and then $i = i_0$.

The second-order moment $M_2 = \frac{1}{M}\sum_{m=0}^{M-1}|U_m|^2$ of the received signal is expressed under the hypotheses $\mathbb{H}_0$ and $\mathbb{H}_1$, respectively, as:

$$M_2 = \begin{cases} \frac{1}{M}\sum_{m=0}^{M-1}|W_m|^2, & \text{if } \mathbb{H}_0 \\ \frac{1}{M}\sum_{m=0}^{M-1}|C_m H_m + W_m|^2, & \text{if } \mathbb{H}_1 \end{cases}. \qquad [3.20]$$

The second-order moment is the decision metric used for the energy-base detector. Here, a different metric noted $\mathcal{M}$ is proposed, and defined by:

$$\mathcal{M} = |M_2 - \hat{\sigma}^2|, \qquad [3.21]$$

where $\hat{\sigma}^2 = \hat{\sigma}^2_{(i_0)}$ is the noise variance estimation performed by means of the iterative algorithm. From [3.20], the metric [3.21] is rewritten according to the hypotheses $\mathbb{H}_0$ and $\mathbb{H}_1$:

$$\mathcal{M} = \begin{cases} |\frac{1}{M}\sum_{m=0}^{M-1}|W_m|^2 - \hat{\sigma}^2|, & \text{under } \mathbb{H}_0 \\ |\frac{1}{M}\sum_{m=0}^{M-1}|C_m H_m + W_m|^2 - \hat{\sigma}^2|, & \text{under } \mathbb{H}_1 \end{cases}. \qquad [3.22]$$

By fixing a threshold ς, the detection and false alarm probabilities are defined by:

$$P_d = P(\mathcal{M} > \varsigma|\mathbb{H}_1) \qquad [3.23]$$

$$P_{fa} = P(\mathcal{M} > \varsigma|\mathbb{H}_0), \qquad [3.24]$$

and the decision criterion is:

$\mathbb{H}_0$, if $\mathcal{M} < \varsigma$

$\mathbb{H}_1$, else.

It is then possible to rewrite the practical algorithm proposed in the scenario of the joint estimation of the SNR and the channel for free band detections, as is summed up in algorithm 3.

---

begin

    Initialization: $\tilde{\mathbf{R}}_H^{LS}$, $e_\sigma > 0$, $\hat{\sigma}_{(i=0)}^2$ and ς ;

    $i \leftarrow 1$;

    while $|\hat{\sigma}_{(i)}^2 - \hat{\sigma}_{(i-1)}^2| > e_\sigma$ **do**

        if $i = 1$ **then**

            Perform LMMSE channel estimation ;

            Perform the noise variance estimation ;

            Calculate the matrix $\tilde{\mathbf{R}}_H^{LMMSE}$;

        else

            Perform an LMMSE channel estimation with $\tilde{\mathbf{R}}_H^{LMMSE}$;

            Perform the noise variance estimation ;

        end

        $i \leftarrow i + 1$;

    end

    Calculate the metric $\mathcal{M}$;

    if $\mathcal{M} < \varsigma$ **then**

        return $\mathbb{H}_0$;

    else

        return $\mathbb{H}_1$;

        Estimate the SNR $\hat{\rho}$ (2.36) with $\hat{\sigma}_{(i_0)}^2$;

    end

end

Algorithm 3. *Application of the MMSE-based algorithm to free band detection*

It can be seen that the structure of algorithm 3 is the same as algorithm 2, but with a detection part. Thus, compared to the methods of the literature, the proposed method returns not only the decision $\mathbb{H}_0$ and $\mathbb{H}_1$, but also:

– the noise variance estimation, if $\mathbb{H}_0$;

– the channel and SNR estimations, if $\mathbb{H}_1$.

An *a priori* qualitative analysis of the detector can be done. Indeed, from [3.22], we can deduce that, by supposing a good estimation of $\hat{\sigma}^2$, $\mathcal{M}$ tends to a value close to zero under $\mathbb{H}_0$, and a value close to P_s under $\mathbb{H}_1$. By supposing a normalized signal power, we can suppose that choosing a value ς between zero and one allows to get a good detector. Concerning the value of the threshold e_σ, since it ensures the convergence of the algorithm, it has no effect on the detector performance. This property will later be shown by simulations.

In the context of cognitive radio, the SUs have to target a given detection probability, denoted as P_d^t. Thus, according to the Neyman–Pearson criterion [KAY 98], the best value of the threshold ς can be analytically derived (when it is possible) by solving $P(\mathcal{M} > \varsigma | \mathbb{H}_1) \geq P_d^t$, and by maximizing the likelihood ratio test (LRT):

$$\Lambda(x) = \frac{p(x|\mathbb{H}_1)}{p(x|\mathbb{H}_0)} \gtrless_{\mathbb{H}_0}^{\mathbb{H}_1} \varsigma. \qquad [3.25]$$

To this end, the probability density functions (PDFs) of $\mathcal{M}$ have to be expressed as proposed in the next section.

3.3. Analytical expressions of the detection and false alarm probabilities

3.3.1. *Probability density function of* $\mathcal{M}$ *under* $\mathbb{H}_1$

From the second line in [3.22], the metric $\mathcal{M}$ is simply expressed as follows:

$$\mathcal{M} = \sum_{l=0}^{L-1} |h_l|^2, \text{ under } \mathbb{H}_1. \qquad [3.26]$$

PROOF.– Under the hypothesis $\mathbb{H}_1$, it is reasonable to suppose that the noise variance estimation is good enough to consider that $\hat{\sigma}^2 \approx \frac{1}{M} \sum_{m=0}^{M-1} |W_m|^2$ from the results of the section 2.2, so the contribution of $C_m H_m$ is prevailing in $\mathcal{M}$ such that:

$$\mathcal{M} = |\frac{1}{M} \sum_{m=0}^{M-1} (|C_m H_m + W_m|^2) - \hat{\sigma}^2|$$

$$= |\frac{1}{M} \sum_{m=0}^{M-1} (|C_m H_m|^2 + |W_m|^2 + CF_m) - \hat{\sigma}^2|, \qquad [3.27]$$

where $\forall m = 0, .., M - 1$, CF_m are the cross factors $(C_m H_m W_m^*)$ + $(C_m H_m W_m^*)^*$, whose mean (for a sufficiently large value of M) is equal to zero, since H_m and W_m are zero-mean uncorrelated Gaussian processes. The development of [3.27] then simply yields:

$$\mathcal{M} = |\frac{1}{M} \sum_{m=0}^{M-1} |C_m H_m|^2 + |W_m|^2 - \hat{\sigma}^2|$$

$$= \frac{1}{M} \sum_{m=0}^{M-1} |H_m C_m|^2, \qquad [3.28]$$

such as $\mathcal{M}$ is linked to the signal power P_s by $P_s = E\{\mathcal{M}\}$. The result in [3.28] obtained with the approximation $\hat{\sigma}^2 \approx \frac{1}{M} \sum_{m=0}^{M-1} |W_m|^2$ can be matter of debate, since it has been seen in section 2.2 that the noise estimation under hypothesis $\mathbb{H}_1$ is biased. However, it will be shown in section 3.4 that this approximation is valid, especially for low values of σ^2. Thus, the developments keeps going on from [3.28]. Whatever $m = 0, .., M - 1$, the mth sample of the channel frequency response given by [1.15] is recalled as:

$$H_m = \sum_{l=0}^{L-1} h_{l,n} \exp(-2j\pi \frac{m}{M} \beta_l). \qquad [3.29]$$

When $C_m C_m^* = 1$, the metric [3.28] can be rewritten as:

$$\mathcal{M} = \frac{1}{M} \sum_{m=0}^{M-1} \left| \sum_{l=0}^{L-1} h_l \exp(-2j\pi \frac{m\beta_l}{M}) C_m \right|^2$$

$$= \frac{1}{M} \sum_{m=0}^{M-1} \left(\sum_{l=0}^{L-1} h_l \exp(-2j\pi \frac{m\beta_l}{M}) C_m \right)$$

$$\times \left(\sum_{l=0}^{L-1} h_l \exp(-2j\pi \frac{m\beta_l}{M}) C_m \right)^*$$

$$= \sum_{l=0}^{L-1} |h_l|^2 + \frac{1}{M} \sum_{m=0}^{M-1} \sum_{l_1=0}^{L-1} \sum_{\substack{l_2=0 \\ l_2 \neq l_1}}^{L-1} h_{l_1} h_{l_2}^* \exp\left(-2j\pi \frac{m(\beta_{l_1} - \beta_{l_2})}{M} \right).$$

$$[3.30]$$

According to the Rayleigh distributed wide sense stationary uncorrelated scattering (WSSUS) channel model, whatever $l = 0, .., L - 1$, the gains h_l are uncorrelated zero mean Gaussian processes. For a large enough value M, let us assume that the mean of the cross factors on the right side of [3.30] is equal to zero. □

From [3.26], it can be seen that $\mathcal{M}$ follows a chi-square distribution with $2L$ degrees of liberty. The PDF, denoted as $p_\mathcal{M}(x)$, of the decision statistic under $\mathbb{H}_1$ is then expressed as:

$$p_\mathcal{M}(x) = \frac{1}{2^L P_s^L \Gamma(L)} x^{L-1} \exp\left(-\frac{x}{2P_s} \right), \quad \text{under } \mathbb{H}_1, \quad [3.31]$$

where $\Gamma(.)$ is the gamma function [ABR 70]. Figure 3.3(a) displays $p_\mathcal{M}(x)$ under $\mathbb{H}_1$.

REMARK 3.1.– $\mathcal{M}$ would exactly follow a chi-square distribution with $2L$ degrees of liberty if all the paths gains $|h_l|^2$ had the same variance. In practice, the paths gains have different variances, so [3.31] is an approximation of a generalized chi-square distribution. As a matter of fact, neither closed-form nor approximation of this distribution has been developped, to our knowledge.

3.3.2. *Probability density function of $\mathcal{M}$ under $\mathbb{H}_0$*

The theoretical expression under the hypothesis $\mathbb{H}_0$ of the PDF of the metric is now derived as:

$$\mathcal{M} = |\frac{1}{M}\sum_{m=0}^{M-1}|W_m|^2 - \hat{\sigma}_{(i)}^2|.$$

To this end, let us assume that the initialization value of the algorithm is chosen large enough to allow the approximation $\hat{\sigma}^2 \approx \sigma^2$, which suits both hypotheses. Whatever $m = 0, ..., M - 1$, each sample W_m is a zero-mean Gaussian process with variance σ^2, $|W_m|^2$ has a chi-square distribution χ_2^2 with a degree of liberty equal to two:

$$\chi_2^2(x) = \frac{1}{\sigma^2}e^{-\frac{x}{\sigma^2}}.$$
[3.32]

The mean and the variance of this distribution are equal to σ^2 and σ^4, respectively. In an OFDM context, we reasonably suppose that M is large enough (e.g. $M > 100$) to consider that, from the central limit theorem, $\frac{1}{M}\sum_{m=0}^{M-1}|W_m|^2$ has a normal distribution $\mathcal{N} \sim (\sigma^2, \frac{\sigma^4}{M})$, and then $\frac{1}{M}\sum_{m=0}^{M-1}|W_m|^2 - \hat{\sigma}^2$ has a centered normal distribution $\mathcal{N} \sim (0, \frac{\sigma^4}{M})$. Consequently, the metric $\mathcal{M} = |\frac{1}{M}\sum_{m=0}^{M-1}|W_m|^2 - \hat{\sigma}_{(i)}^2|$ has a chi-square distribution χ_1 with one degree of liberty:

$$p_{\mathcal{M}}(x) = \frac{\sqrt{2}}{\Gamma(\frac{1}{2})\sqrt{\sigma^4/M}}\exp\left(-\frac{1}{2}(\frac{x}{\sqrt{\sigma^4/M}})^2\right), \text{under } \mathbb{H}_0 \quad [3.33]$$

The PDFs of the metric $\mathcal{M}$, according to $\mathbb{H}_0$ and $\mathbb{H}_1$:

$$p_{\mathcal{M}}(x) = \begin{cases} \dfrac{\sqrt{2}}{\Gamma(\frac{1}{2})\sqrt{\sigma^4/M}}\exp\left(-\frac{1}{2}(\frac{x}{\sqrt{\sigma^4/M}})^2\right), & \text{under } \mathbb{H}_0 \\ \dfrac{1}{2^L P_s^L \Gamma(L)} x^{L-1}\exp\left(-\frac{x}{2P_s}\right), & \text{under } \mathbb{H}_1 \end{cases}$$ [3.34]

are depicted in Figure 3.3(b) using the following parameters: $L = 4$, $P_s = \sigma^2 = 1$ and $M = 148$.

3.3.3. *Analytical expressions of P_d and P_{fa}*

The detection and false alarm probabilities P_d and P_{fa} are obtained by integrating [3.34] between the fixed level ς and $+\infty$. For the calculation of P_d, the solution is given in [KOS 02] and [DIG 07]:

$$P_d = P(\mathcal{M} > \varsigma | \mathbb{H}_1)$$

$$= \int_{\varsigma}^{+\infty} \frac{x^{L-1}}{2^L P_s^L \Gamma(L)} \exp\left(-\frac{x}{2P_s}\right) dx$$

$$= \frac{\Gamma(L, \frac{\varsigma}{2P_s})}{\Gamma(L)},$$ [3.35]

where $\Gamma(.,.)$ is the incomplete gamma function [ABR 70]. In the case $\mathbb{H}_0$, we have:

$$P_{fa} = P(\mathcal{M} > \varsigma | \mathcal{H}_0)$$

$$= \int_{\varsigma}^{+\infty} p_{\mathcal{M}}(x) dx$$

$$= \int_{\varsigma}^{+\infty} \frac{\sqrt{2}}{\Gamma(\frac{1}{2})\sqrt{\sigma^4/M}} e^{-\frac{1}{2}(\frac{x}{\sqrt{\sigma^4/M}})^2} dx.$$ [3.36]

By using the change of variable $X = \dfrac{x}{\sqrt{2\sigma^4/M}}$, and given that $\Gamma(\frac{1}{2}) = \sqrt{\pi}$, we recognize the complementary error function $erfc(x) = 1 - erf(x)$:

$$P_{fa} = \int_{\frac{\varsigma}{\sqrt{2\sigma^4/M}}}^{+\infty} \frac{2}{\sqrt{\pi}} e^{-X^2} dX$$

$$= erfc(\frac{\varsigma\sqrt{M}}{\sqrt{2}\sigma^2}). \qquad\qquad [3.37]$$

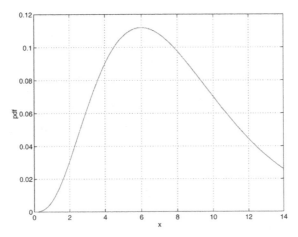

a) Pdf $p_{\mathcal{M}}(x)$ under $\mathbb{H}_0$

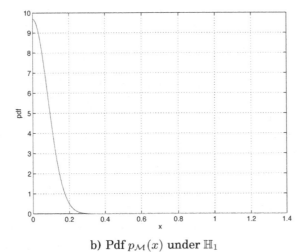

b) Pdf $p_{\mathcal{M}}(x)$ under $\mathbb{H}_1$

Figure 3.3. $p_{\mathcal{M}}(x)$ *under hypotheses* $\mathbb{H}_0$ *and* $\mathbb{H}_1$

Since the incomplete gamma function is not directly invertible in [3.35], it is not possible to derive an analytical expression of the threshold ς function of the target detection probability P_d^t. However, an approximation by means of a computer calculation or a series expansion of the inverse of [3.35], or a simple characterization of ς by simulations can be done. We will consider this third solution thereafter. Furthermore, the next section aims to characterize the performance of the proposed detection algorithm, and the validity of the proposed analytical developments.

3.4. Simulations results

The parameters remain the same as the ones used for the theoretical and the practical approaches of the algorithm in the previous chapter.

3.4.1. *Choice of the threshold ς*

Figure 3.4 depicts the metric $\mathcal{M} = |M_2 - \hat{\sigma}^2|$ versus the number of iterations, under the hypotheses $\mathbb{H}_0$ and $\mathbb{H}_1$. The SNR is fixed equal to 0 dB. In presence of a signal, the average signal power P_s is equal to 1. The curves are obtained after to 4,000 simulation runs.

It can be seen that the *a priori* qualitative analysis is verified. Indeed, for a sufficient number of iterations (according to the value e_σ, as shown thereafter), $\mathcal{M}$ converges to P_s under $\mathbb{H}_1$, and converges to zero under $\mathbb{H}_0$. It has been noticed that it is not possible to find an exact value of ς according to $P(\mathcal{M} > \varsigma | \mathbb{H}_1) = P_d^t$. However, it can be observed in Figure 3.4 that the choice of the threshold is not restricting. Indeed, choosing ς as small as desired ensures a probability P_d close to one, and, for a sufficient number of iterations, it also ensures a low value for P_{fa}. However, reducing the value of e_σ increases the number of required iterations, as shown later. For an expected detection probability, a trade-off between the complexity and the acceptable level of false alarm probability has to be taken into account.

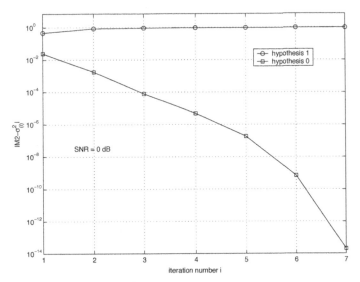

Figure 3.4. $|M_2 - \hat{\sigma}^2|$ *versus the iterations number under* $\mathbb{H}_0$ *and* $\mathbb{H}_1$, *for SNR = 0 dB*

3.4.2. *Effect of the choice of* e_σ *on the detector performance*

In this section, it is shown that the value of the threshold e_σ has no effect on the detection performance of the proposed method, but only plays a role on the speed of convergence of the algorithm. Figure 3.5 depicts the curves of probabilities of detection P_d and false alarm P_{fa} versus the SNR from −15 dB to 10 dB. In order to ensure the convergence of the algorithm, e_σ must have a low value. Figures 3.5(a) and (b) then depict the curves P_d and P_{fa} for $e_\sigma = 0.01$ and $e_\sigma = 0.0001$, respectively. According to these recommendations, the initialization $\sigma^2_{(i=0)}$ is equal to $40 \times M_2$. Also, we arbitrarily fix the threshold $\varsigma = 0.01$, its effect on the detection performance being further studied. The figures are obtained after to 2,000 simulation runs.

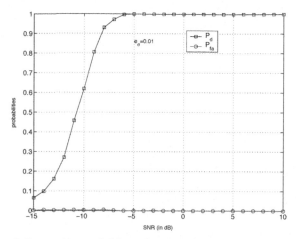

a) Detection and false alarm probabilities P_d and P_{fa} versus SNR, for $e_\sigma = 0.01$

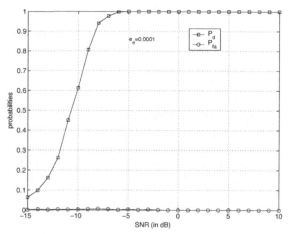

b) Detection and false alarm probabilities P_d and P_{fa} versus SNR, for $e_\sigma = 0.0001$

Figure 3.5. *Detection and false alarm probabilities in function of SNR, for two values of e_σ and for a fixed value $\varsigma = 0.01$*

We observe that the curves of both P_d and P_{fa} have the same shape on Figures 3.5(a) and (b). P_{fa} is equal to zero or nearly zero for all SNR values and P_d reaches one from SNR = -5 dB. The detector can then reach a perfect one from $SNR \geq -5$ dB, i.e. in low SNR environment. We conclude that, assuming a value of e_σ small enough to ensure the convergence of the algorithm, this threshold does not have any effect on the detection performance of the proposed method.

Figure 3.6 displays the number of iterations the algorithm needs before it stops versus the SNR from -10 to 10 dB. We consider three different values for the threshold: $e_\sigma = 0.01$, $e_\sigma = 0.001$ and $e_\sigma = 0.0001$. The conditions of simulations remain the same.

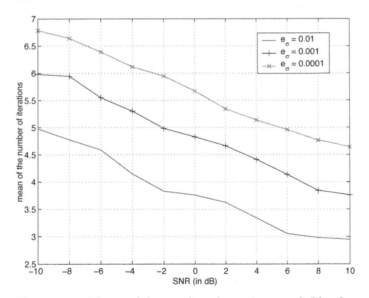

Figure 3.6. *Means of the number of iterations needed by the algorithm to stop versus SNR (in dB), for three values of threshold e_σ*

Although the Figures 3.5(a) and (b) present almost the same probabilities whatever the threshold e_σ, they differ from each other in the number of iterations the algorithm requires before stopping. Indeed, remembering that we compare $|\hat{\sigma}^2_{(i)} - \hat{\sigma}^2_{(i-1)}|$ with e_σ, the lower the e_σ, the larger the number of iterations i needed to reach e_σ. However, Figure 3.6 shows that the maximum mean of iterations is less than seven for SNR = -10 dB and shows the maximum mean of iterations is less than five for SNR = -10 dB and $e_\sigma = 0.0001$, which is a reasonable number of iterations. We conclude that the choice of e_σ has no effect on the detector efficiency, while it allows the convergence of the algorithm. Furthermore, the number of required iterations reasonably increases when e_σ and SNR have low values. The detector then remains usable in practice under these conditions.

3.4.3. Detector performance under non-WSS channel model and synchronization mismatch

In this section, we study the behavior of the proposed detector when a non-wide sense stationary (WSS) channel is considered, and when the receiver is not synchronized with the received signal, as in Figure 1.4.

To simulate a non-WSS channel, we artificially correlate the different paths h_l with $l = 1, .., L - 1$ with h_0 by inserting the gain h_0 into the other path gains. Thus, from the original channel impulse response $[h_0, .., h_{L-1}]$ with independent paths, we build a new correlated vector $[h_0, .., \tilde{h}_l, .., \tilde{h}_{L-1}]$ such as, for $l = 1, .., L - 1$, we define $\tilde{h}_l$ as:

$$\tilde{h}_l = h_l + \alpha_l h_0, \qquad\qquad [3.38]$$

where α_l is a real coefficient that is calculated as a function of the expected correlation coefficient ρ_h that is expressed as:

$$\rho_h = \frac{E\{h_0 \tilde{h}_l^*\}}{\sigma_0 \tilde{\sigma}_l}, \qquad\qquad [3.39]$$

where σ_0^2 and $\tilde{\sigma}_l^2$ are the variances of h_0 and $\tilde{h}_l$, respectively. Figure 3.7 displays the detection probability P_d versus the

SNR when correlation between the paths is considered. Three curves are considered: the reference ($\rho_h = 0$), two correlated channels with $\rho_h = 0.1$ and $\rho_h = 0.5$. We observe a limited gap of 1 dB between the reference curve and the two others. We conclude that the proposed detector is robust against the channel uncertainty.

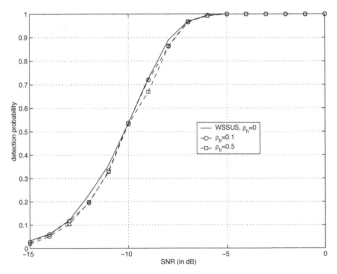

Figure 3.7. *Detection probability versus SNR for a non-WSS channel*

Figure 3.8 displays detection probability curves as functions of the SNR and for different time gap values δ. The synchronization mismatch is given as a percentage of the OFDM symbol duration δ/Ts. We focus on the detection probability because in a cognitive radio context, it must be as large as possible.

A loss of performance caused by the synchronization mismatch up to 7 dB for δ/Ts =20% can be observed in Figure 3.8. This arises from the interference term $\mathbf{I}(\delta)$ in [3.2] that reduces the signal to interference and noise ratio value. However, a fixed synchronization mismatch corresponding to a constant time offset of the acquisition window and the effective signal (see Figure 1.4) is considered. Indeed, as $\delta > 0$ this is the worst situation since the CP cannot be exploited to retrieve the missing OFDM symbol. A solution to improve the detection probability under synchronization mismatch condition consists of using the algorithm during several consecutive symbols. However, this alternative would probably increase the complexity of the detector and would also increase the sensing time, initially equal to 1 OFDM time duration.

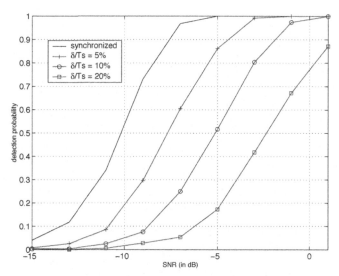

Figure 3.8. *Detection probability versus SNR for different values of* δ/Ts

3.4.4. *Receiver operating characteristic of the detector*

The performance of a detector is usually evaluated by means of the receiver operating characteristic (ROC) curves, depicting the detection probability P_d function of the false alarm probability P_{fa}. The optimal detector is logically reached at the point $(P_{fa} = 0, P_d = 1)$. The curve $P_{fa} = P_d$ is called line of chance, and corresponds to a detector which makes as much good decisions as false alarms. If the ROC curve is above the first bisector, the detector is qualified as efficient, since $P_d > P_{fa}$.

Figure 3.9 compares the ROC curves of the proposed detector given by simulation with the theoretical curves P_d and P_{fa} given by [3.35] and [3.37], respectively. It can be observed that the theoretical curve for SNR = 0 dB is very close to the curve obtained by simulation, whereas for SNR = −10 dB, the difference is more noticeable. This observation tallies with the discussion on the approximation $\hat{\sigma}^2 \approx \frac{1}{M} \sum_{m=0}^{M-1} |W_m|^2$ in the calculation of the metric $\mathcal{M}$ under the hypothesis $\mathbb{H}_1$. Indeed, this approximation is justified for high values of SNR, but becomes wrong for the very low SNR values. Besides this, we remarked that the PDF of $\mathcal{M}$ in [3.31] is not rigorously exact, since no closed-form expression of a generalized chi-square distribution exists in the literature. However, the theoretical curves allow us to give an idea on the detector performance for a given SNR, even for the low SNR values.

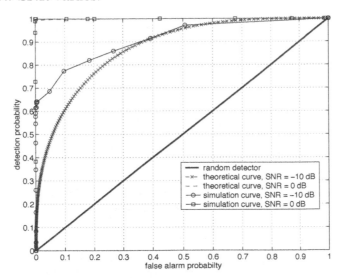

Figure 3.9. *Comparison of the receiver operating characteristic (ROC) curves obtained by simulation and in theory. For a color version of the figure, see www.iste.co.uk / savaux / mmse.zip*

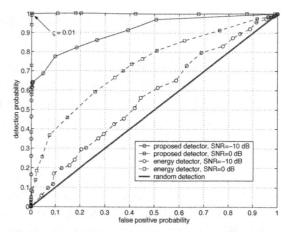

a) Proposed detector compared with the energy detector

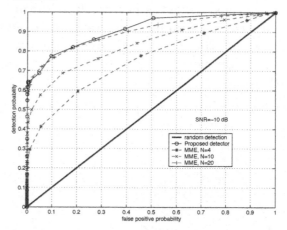

b) Proposed detector compared with the MME detector

Figure 3.10. *Receiver operating characteristic (ROC) curves of the proposed method compared to the energy detector a) and MME detector b)*

Figure 3.10 shows the ROC curves of the proposed detector for low SNR values: SNR = -10 dB and SNR = 0 dB. The conditions of simulation remain the same, and we fix the threshold at e_σ = 0.01. The proposed detector is also compared to the usual energy detector, whose metric $\mathcal{M}$ is equal to the second-order moment of the received signal M_2. This metric is compared to the threshold ς to obtain the following decision rule:

$\mathbb{H}_0$,   if $\mathcal{M} < \varsigma$

$\mathbb{H}_1$,   else.

In Figure 3.10(b), the proposed detector is compared to the usual MME detector, whose metric $\mathcal{M}'$ is equal to the ratio of the maximum and the non-zero minimum eigenvalues of the received signal covariance matrix $\check{\mathbf{R}}$, i.e. $\mathcal{M}' = \lambda_{max}/\lambda_{min}$. The same aforementioned decision rule is used. Since a single input single output (SISO) system is assumed, $\check{\mathbf{R}}$ is obtained by concatenating N consecutive OFDM symbols so that $\underline{\mathbf{U}}_N = [\mathbf{U}_1, .., \mathbf{U}_N]$ and then $\check{\underline{\mathbf{R}}} = \underline{\mathbf{U}}_N \underline{\mathbf{U}}_N^T$. In that way, $\underline{\mathbf{U}}_N$ is equivalent to a system with N sensors. However, due to the nature of the channel, the different OFDM symbols received are correlated. In Figure 3.10(b), the ROC curves of MME are obtained for N = 4,10 and 20 symbols, and the SNR is equal to −10 dB. Each point of the curves is obtained by means of 2,000 simulation runs.

It can be seen in Figure 3.10(a) that the proposed detector outperforms the energy detector, whatever the SNR value. Indeed, as we consider the detection of a preamble transmitted over a Rayleigh channel, the power of the received signal P_S in [3.27] is not constant and follows a chi-square distribution. Consequently, for simulations made at a fixed SNR, the noise variance is also a varying process, which deteriorates the detector performance. For additional details about the theoretical development of the energy detection of signals with random amplitude, please refer to [KOS 02, DIG 07]. We may also explain the performance of our detector by the fact that we use the same sensing time to compare the energy detector and the proposed algorithm, i.e. only one OFDM symbol length. The 148 samples of one

OFDM symbol is not enough to obtain an accurate energy detector. Figure 3.10(a) also confirms that the proposed detector is very efficient, since it is able to reach the perfect detector for $\varsigma = 0.01$. Indeed, for SNR = 0 dB, we observe that the ROC curve reaches the point $(P_{fa} = 0, P_d = 1)$, as we mentioned in Figures 3.5(a) and (b) for $SNR \geq -5$ dB. In Figure 3.10(b), we observe that MME requires $N = 20$ symbols to reach the performance of the proposed method, because MME is efficient for a very large size of $\underline{\mathbf{U}}_N$, and the vectors of the latter matrix are correlated. Thus, for a given performance, the complexity of MME is $\mathcal{O}(NM^2)$ (for the computation and the diagonalization of $\check{\mathbf{R}}$) and the one of the proposed algorithms is $\mathcal{O}(i_f M^3)$. Since we reasonably have $N < i_f M$, we conclude that the iterative method is more complex than the usual second-order moment-based techniques. However, in addition to the detection process, the proposed algorithm performs the noise variance estimation if H_0 and the SNR and channel estimation if H_1, which is an advantage by comparison with the techniques of the literature.

3.5. Summary

In this chapter, an application of the MMSE-based channel and noise estimator to spectrum sensing has been presented. It has been shown that in presence of noise only, the algorithm accurately estimates the noise variance. Therefore, the absolute difference between the measured signal power and the estimated noise variance is proposed as a metric. The detection and false alarm probabilities have been analytically derived, thanks to a few approximations, and the performance of the method is evaluated through simulations. It has been shown that, compared to the usual radiometer and the MME detector, the proposed algorithm has a very good trade-off between the sensing duration and the performance.

Conclusion

In this work, an iterative MMSE-based method for the joint detection of an OFDM signal and the estimation of the multipath channel and the noise variance has been detailed. In Chapter 1, the system model, the notations were presented and some basics elements concerning the transmission of an OFDM signal over a multipath channel were recalled. In Chapters 2 and 3, the algorithm for the noise variance and the channel estimation, and its application to the signal detection were presented respectively. Figure C.1 depicts the general principle of the proposed technique: whatever the input $\hat{\mathbf{H}}^{LS}$ (signal and noise or noise only), the structure of the algorithm remains the same and returns $\mathbb{H}_1, \hat{\sigma}^2, \hat{\mathbf{H}}^{LMMSE}$ in the presence of a signal and $\mathbb{H}_0, \hat{\sigma}^2$ in the absence of a signal in the sensed band.

This multiple use of the algorithm with a unique structure is very interesting, in particular in a cognitive radio context. Indeed, it provides a practical solution for three key elements in a transmission chain: the signal detection for an opportunistic spectrum access, the measure of the noise level in the band, and an accurate channel estimation. Thus, although the MMSE-based method has a high computational cost, the proposed algorithm requires a sole computation block in a device instead of three. Moreover, several ways of reduction of the technique complexity and an application of the method to other multi-carrier modulations (e.g. OFDM/Offset-QAM) are possible.

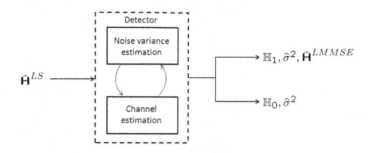

Figure C.1. *Diagram of the proposed algorithm, usable as a detector and an estimator*

Appendix 1

Appendix to Chapter 2

This appendix aims to prove that the algorithm converges toward zero when it is performed with only $\tilde{\mathbf{R}}_H^{LS}$ under hypothesis $\mathbb{H}_1$. It justifies the substitution of this matrix by $\tilde{\mathbf{R}}_H^{LMMSE}$ for $i \geq 2$. If the steps [2.31] and [2.32] are performed with $\tilde{\mathbf{R}}_H^{LS}$, then it yields:

$$
\begin{aligned}
\hat{\sigma}_{(i+1)}^2 &= \frac{1}{M} E\{\|\hat{\mathbf{H}}^{LS} - \hat{\mathbf{H}}_{(i+1)}^{LMMSE}\|^2\} \\
&= \frac{1}{M} tr\left(\hat{\sigma}_{(i)}^4 (\tilde{\mathbf{R}}_H^{LS} + \hat{\sigma}_{(i)}^2 \mathbf{I})^{-1}(\underline{\mathbf{R}}_H + \sigma^2 \underline{\mathbf{I}}) \right. \\
&\quad \left. \times ((\tilde{\mathbf{R}}_H^{LS} + \hat{\sigma}_{(i)}^2 I)^{-1})^H\right).
\end{aligned}
\tag{A1.1}
$$

We recall that for a large value M, $\frac{1}{M} tr(\tilde{\mathbf{R}}_H^{LS}) = \frac{1}{M} tr(\underline{\mathbf{R}}_H + \sigma^2 \underline{\mathbf{I}})$, so let us assume that in a first approximation, $\tilde{\mathbf{R}}_H^{LS} = \underline{\mathbf{R}}_H + \sigma^2 \underline{\mathbf{I}}$ in order to develop [A1.1]:

$$
\begin{aligned}
\hat{\sigma}_{(i+1)}^2 &= \frac{1}{M} tr\left(\hat{\sigma}_{(i)}^4 (\underline{\mathbf{R}}_H + (\hat{\sigma}_{(i)}^2 + \sigma^2)\mathbf{I})^{-1}(\underline{\mathbf{R}}_H + \sigma^2 \underline{\mathbf{I}}) \right. \\
&\quad \left. \times ((\underline{\mathbf{R}}_H + (\hat{\sigma}_{(i)}^2 + \sigma^2)\underline{\mathbf{I}})^{-1})^H\right).
\end{aligned}
\tag{A1.2}
$$

$\mathbf{R}_H$ being an Hermitian matrix, it is possible to take the same diagonalization property given in [SAV 12] and in section 2.1 for the expression [A1.2], hence the scalar form of [A1.2] is written as:

$$\hat{\sigma}^2_{(i+1)} = \frac{\hat{\sigma}^4_{(i)}}{M} \sum_{m=0}^{M-1} \frac{\lambda_m + \sigma^2}{(\lambda_m + \sigma^2 + \hat{\sigma}^2_{(i)})^2}, \qquad [\text{A1.3}]$$

where λ_m are the eigenvalues of the covariance matrix $\underline{\mathbf{R}}_H$.

PROPOSITION A1.1.– $\forall \lambda_m, \sigma^2 \in \mathbb{R}$ and $M \in \mathbb{N}$,

$$\lim_{i \to \infty} \hat{\sigma}^2_{(i)} = 0, \qquad [\text{A1.4}]$$

with $(\hat{\sigma}^2_{(i)})$ as defined in [A1.3].

PROOF.– If we note $x = \hat{\sigma}^2_{(i)}$, the sequence $(\hat{\sigma}^2_{(i+1)})$ is built from a function f_{r1} such that

$$f_{r1}(x) = \frac{x^2}{M} \sum_{m=0}^{M-1} \frac{\lambda_m + \sigma^2}{(\lambda_m + \sigma^2 + x)^2}, \qquad [\text{A1.5}]$$

with $x \in [0, +\infty[$. The proof of the convergence of the sequence $(\hat{\sigma}^2_{(i+1)})$ in [A1.3] toward zero is based on the fixed-point theorem, i.e. we show that the only solution to the equation $f_{r1}(x) = x$ is zero. The limits of f_{r1} are $f_{r1}(0) = 0$ and $\lim_{x \to \infty} f_1(x) = \frac{1}{M} \sum_{m=0}^{M-1} (\lambda_m + \sigma^2) = M_2$. Furthermore, the derivative of f_{r1}

$$f'_{r1}(x) = \frac{2x}{M} \sum_{m=0}^{M-1} \frac{(\lambda_m + \sigma^2)^2}{(\lambda_m + \sigma^2 + x)^3}, \qquad [\text{A1.6}]$$

is positive for $x \in [0, +\infty[$, so f_{r1} is increasing on this interval. We then deduce the inclusion $f_{r1}([0, +\infty[) \subset [0, M_2]$ and so $f_{r1}([0, M_2]) \subset [0, M_2]$. Thus, f_{r1} has at least one fixed point on

$[0, M_2]$. As f_{r1} is increasing on $[0, M_2]$, we conclude that the sequence $(\hat{\sigma}^2_{(i+1)})$ converges to one of the fixed points of f_{r1}. An obvious fixed point of f_{r1} is zero, since $f_{r1}(0) = 0$. We now prove that 0 is the sole fixed point of f_{r1} on $[0, M_2]$. To this end, we show that $f'_{r1}(x) < 1$, which is equivalent to $(f_{r1}(x) - x)' < 0$. Let us define the function $f_{r1m}(x)$ extracted from $f_{r1}(x)$ so that $f_{r1}(x) = \frac{1}{M}\sum_m^{M-1} f_{r1m}(x)$:

$$f_{r1m}(x) = \frac{x^2(\lambda_m + \sigma^2)}{(\lambda_m + \sigma^2 + x)^2}. \qquad [A1.7]$$

Since f_{r1} is defined by a sum, the derivative $f'_{r1}(x)$ is a sum of the derivative $f'_{r1m}(x)$ as well, with:

$$f'_{r1m}(x) = \frac{2x(\lambda_m + \sigma^2)^2}{(\lambda_m + \sigma^2 + x)^3}. \qquad [A1.8]$$

For any value of $m = 0, 1, ..., M - 1$ and $x \geq 0$, we have $f'_{r1m}(x) \geq 0$, so the following triangle inequality on the derivative of f_{r1} is applied as:

$$\max_x(f'_{r1}(x)) \leq \frac{1}{M}\sum_{m=0}^{M-1} \max_{x,m}(f'_{r1m}(x)). \qquad [A1.9]$$

For $m = 0, 1, ..., M - 1$, we find the maximum of $f'_{r1m}(x)$ due to a second derivation such that:

$$f''_{r1m}(x) = \frac{2(\lambda_m + \sigma^2)^2(\lambda_m + \sigma^2 - 2x)}{(\lambda_m + \sigma^2 + x)^4}. \qquad [A1.10]$$

The second derivative of $f_{r1m}(x)$ in [A1.10] is null for $x = \frac{1}{2}(\lambda_m + \sigma^2)$, so, with the help of expression [A1.8] we find that:

$$\max_x(f'_{r1m}(x)) = f'_{r1m}(x = \frac{1}{2}(\lambda_m + \sigma^2)) = \frac{8}{27}. \qquad [A1.11]$$

Equation [A1.11] shows that for any value of $m = 0, 1, ..., M - 1$, the maximum of f'_{r1_m} is equal to $\frac{8}{27}$, so the triangle inequality is simplified as:

$$\max_x(f'_{r1}(x)) \leq \frac{8}{27}, \qquad\qquad \text{[A1.12]}$$

which then proves that $f'_{r1}(x) < 1$, i.e. f has only one fixed point equal to zero. Figure A1.1 shows examples of $f_{r1}(x)$ and $f'_{r1}(x)$. We can conclude that if the algorithm is performed with the covariance matrix $\tilde{\mathbf{R}}_H^{LS}$, then the sequence $(\hat{\sigma}^2_{(i)})$ converges to zero and the algorithm enters into an endless loop, whatever the value of the initialization $\hat{\sigma}^2_{(0)}$.   □

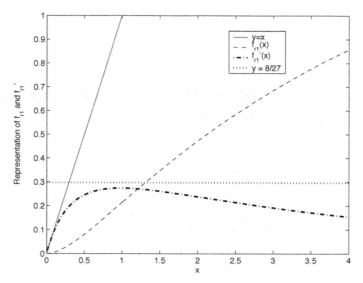

Figure A1.1. *Shape of $f_{r1}(x)$, $f'_{r1}(x)$ compared to $y = x$ and $y = 8/27$*

Appendix 2

Appendix to Chapter 3

This appendix aims to prove that the algorithm converges toward zero when it is performed with only $\tilde{\underline{\mathbf{R}}}_H^{LS}$ under hypothesis $\mathbb{H}_0$. Thus, we deduce the scalar expression of the algorithm from the step 4 in section 3.2.2:

Perform the LMMSE channel estimation:

$$\hat{\mathbf{H}}_{(i+1)}^{LMMSE} = \tilde{\underline{\mathbf{R}}}_H^{LS}(\tilde{\underline{\mathbf{R}}}_H^{LS} + \hat{\sigma}_{(i)}^2\underline{\mathbf{I}})^{-1}\hat{\mathbf{H}}^{LS}. \qquad \text{[A2.1]}$$

Perform the MMSE noise variance estimation:

$$\hat{\sigma}_{(i+1)}^2 = \frac{1}{M}E\{||\hat{\mathbf{H}}^{LS} - \hat{\mathbf{H}}_{(i+1)}^{LMMSE}||_F^2\}. \qquad \text{[A2.2]}$$

It is assumed that M is large enough to get $tr(\mathbf{W}\mathbf{W}^H) = tr(\sigma^2\mathbf{I})$ so we write, in first approximation, $\tilde{\underline{\mathbf{R}}}_H^{LS} \approx \sigma^2\underline{\mathbf{I}}$. Hence the development of [A2.2] yields:

$$\hat{\sigma}_{(i+1)}^2 = \frac{1}{M}E\{||\hat{\mathbf{H}}^{LS} - \hat{\mathbf{H}}_{(i+1)}^{LMMSE}||_F^2\}$$

$$= \frac{1}{M}E\{||\hat{\mathbf{H}}^{LS} - \tilde{\underline{\mathbf{R}}}_H^{LS}(\tilde{\underline{\mathbf{R}}}_H^{LS} + \hat{\sigma}_{(i)}^2\underline{\mathbf{I}})^{-1}\hat{\mathbf{H}}^{LS}||_F^2\},$$

$$\text{[A2.3]}$$

and, by factorizing by $\underline{\mathbf{C}}^{-1}$:

$$\hat{\sigma}^2_{(i+1)} = \frac{1}{M} E\{||\mathbf{W} - \sigma^2\underline{\mathbf{I}}(\sigma^2\underline{\mathbf{I}} + \hat{\sigma}^2_{(i)}\underline{\mathbf{I}})^{-1}\mathbf{W}||^2_F\}$$

$$= \frac{1}{M} E\{||(\underline{\mathbf{I}} - (\sigma^2 + \hat{\sigma}^2_{(i)} - \hat{\sigma}^2_{(i)})\underline{\mathbf{I}}((\sigma^2 + \hat{\sigma}^2_{(i)})\underline{\mathbf{I}})^{-1})\mathbf{W}||^2_F\}$$

$$= \frac{1}{M} E\{||(\hat{\sigma}^2_{(i)}\underline{\mathbf{I}}((\sigma^2 + \hat{\sigma}^2_{(i)})\underline{\mathbf{I}})^{-1})\mathbf{W}||^2_F\}$$

$$= \frac{\hat{\sigma}^4_{(i)}}{(\sigma^2 + \hat{\sigma}^2_{(i)})^2} \frac{1}{M} E\{||\mathbf{W}||^2_F\}$$

$$= \frac{\hat{\sigma}^4_{(i)}\sigma^2}{(\sigma^2 + \hat{\sigma}^2_{(i)})^2}. \qquad\qquad\qquad\qquad [\text{A2.4}]$$

PROPOSITION A2.1.– $\forall\sigma^2 \in \mathbb{R}$:

$$\lim_{i\to\infty} \hat{\sigma}^2_{(i)} = 0, \qquad\qquad\qquad\qquad\qquad [\text{A2.5}]$$

with $(\hat{\sigma}^2_{(i)})$ as defined in [A2.4].

PROOF.– The sequence $(\hat{\sigma}^2_{(i)})$ is built from a function f_s such that, if we note $x = \hat{\sigma}^2_{(i)}$, we obtain:

$$f_s(x) = \frac{x^2\sigma^2}{(\sigma^2 + x)^2}, \qquad\qquad\qquad\qquad [\text{A2.6}]$$

with $x \in \mathbb{R}^+$. Figure A2.1 displays the curves of f_s for different values of σ^2 and compares them to $y = x$.

The sequence $(\hat{\sigma}^2_{(i)})$ converges if f_s has at least one fixed point, i.e. a solution of the equation $f_s(x) = x$. Obviously, zero is one fixed point. We now show that zero is the only fixed point of f_s. To this end, the first derivative f'_s and the second derivative f''_s of f_s are expressed respectively, as:

$$f'_s(x) = \frac{2\sigma^4 x}{(\sigma^2 + x)^3}, \qquad\qquad\qquad\qquad [\text{A2.7}]$$

and

$$f_s''(x) = \frac{2\sigma^4(\sigma^2 - 2x)}{(\sigma^2 + x)^4}.$$ [A2.8]

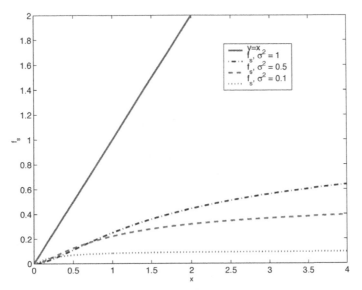

Figure A2.1. *Aspect of f for different values
of σ^2 compared with $y = x$*

From [A2.7], we deduce that $\forall x \in \mathbb{R}^+$, $f_s'(x) \geq 0$, so f_s is increasing on $\mathbb{R}^+$. From [A2.8], we find that $f_s''(x) = 0$ for $x = \frac{\sigma^2}{2}$, then the maximum value of f_s' is $f'(\frac{\sigma^2}{2}) = \frac{8}{81} < 1$. Since $f_s(0) = 0$ and $\max(f_s') = \frac{8}{81} < 1$, we conclude that the only fixed point of f_s is 0. We find the same results as in the case of a received pilot preamble under hypothesis $\mathbb{H}_1$, that is if the algorithm is exclusively performed with $\tilde{\mathbf{R}}_H^{LS}$, then the sole limit to $\hat{\sigma}_{(i+1)}^2$ is zero and the algorithm enters into an endless loop. $\square$

It justifies the change of channel covariance matrix from $\tilde{\mathbf{R}}_H^{LS}$ to $\tilde{\mathbf{R}}_H^{LMMSE}$ under hypothesis $\mathbb{H}_1$ and under hypothesis $\mathbb{H}_0$ as well.

Bibliography

[ABR 70] ABRAMOWITZ M., STEGUN I., "Gamma function and related functions", *Handbook of Mathematical Functions with Formulas, Graphs, and Mathematical Tables*, Chapter 6, Dover, New York, 1970.

[ABU 08] ABUTHINIEN M., CHEN S., HANZO L., "Semi-blind joint maximum likelihood channel estimation and data detection for MIMO systems", *IEEE Signal Processing Letters*, vol. 15, pp. 202–205, 2008.

[AXE 12] AXELL E., LEUS G., LARSSON E.G., *et al.*, "Spectrum sensing for cognitive radio: state-of-the-art and recent advances", *IEEE Signal Processing Magazine*, vol. 29, no. 3, pp. 101–116, May 2012.

[BEL 63] BELLO P., "Characterization of randomly time-variant linear channels", *IEEE Transactions on Communications Systems*, vol. 11, no. 4, pp. 360–393, December 1963.

[BEN 67] BENEDICT T.R., SOONG T.T., "The joint estimation of signal and noise from the sum envelope", *IEEE Transaction on Information Theory*, vol. 13, pp. 447–454, July 1967.

[BIG 04] BIGUESH M., GERSHMAN A.B., "Downlink channel estimation in cellular systems with antenna arrays at base stations using channel probing with feedback", *EURASIP Journal on Applied Signal Processing*, vol. 9, pp. 1330–1339, September 2004.

[BOU 03] BOUMARD S., "Novel noise variance and SNR estimation algorithm for wireless MIMO OFDM systems", *Global Telecommunications Conference*, vol. 3, pp. 1330–1334, December 2003.

[CAR 08] CARDOSO L.S., DEBBAH M., BIANCHI P., *et al.*, "Cooperative spectrum sensing using random matrix theory", *ISWPC*, Santorini, Greece, pp. 334–338, May 2008.

[COL 02] COLERI S., ERGEN M., PURI A., *et al.*, "A study of channel estimation in OFDM systems", *Vehicular Technology Conference Fall*, vol. 2, pp. 894–898, September 2002.

[CON] CONSTANTINI G., Déterminant d'une matrice circulante, http://gilles.constantini.pagesperso-orange.fr/agreg_fichiers/themes_fichiers/detcirc.pdf.

[DEB] DEBBAH M., OFDM, Short introduction to OFDM tutorial, p. 11. Available at http://www.supelec.fr/d2ri/flexibleradio/cours/ofdmtutorial.pdf

[DEM 77] DEMPSTER A.P., LAIRD N.M., RUBIN D.B., "Maximum likelihood from incomplete data via the EM algorithm", *Journal of the Royal Statistical Society. Series B*, vol. 39, no. 1, pp. 1–38, 1977.

[DIG 07] DIGHAM F.F., ALOUINI M.S., SIMON M.K., "On the energy detection of unknown signals over fading channels", *IEEE Transactions on Communications*, vol. 55, no. 1, pp. 21–24, 2007.

[DON 07] DONG X., LU W.-S., SOONG A., "Linear interpolation in pilot symbol assisted channel estimation for OFDM", *IEEE Transactions on Wireless Communications*, vol. 6, no. 5, pp. 1910–1920, May 2007.

[EDF 98] EDFORS O., SANDELL M., VAN DE BEEK J.-J., *et al.*, "OFDM channel estimation by singular value decomposition", *IEEE Transactions on Communications*, vol. 46, no. 7, pp. 931–939, July 1998.

[ETS 04] ETSI, Digital video broadcasting (DVB) framing structure, channel coding and modulation for digital terrestrial television, no. ETSI EN 300 744 V1.5.1, ETSI, 2004.

[ETS 09] ETSI, Digital radio mondiale (DRM); system specification, no. ETSI ES 201 980 V 3.1.1, ETSI, August 2009.

[FOE 01] FOERSTER J.R., "The effects of multipath interference on the performance of UWB systems in an indoor wireless channel", *Vehicular Technology Conference Spring*, vol. 2, Rhodes, pp. 1176–1180, May 2001.

[GAR 91] GARDNER W.A., "Exploitation of spectral redundancy in cyclostationary signals", *IEEE Signal Processing Magazine*, vol. 8, no. 2, pp. 14–36, April 1991.

[GRA 06] GRAY R.M., "Toeplitz and circulant matrices: a review", Department of Electrical Engineering, Standford University, 2006.

[HOE 97] HOEHER P., KAISER S., ROBERTSON P., "Two-dimensional pilot-symbol-aided channel estimation by Wiener filtering", *ICASSP*, Munich, vol. 3,pp. 1845–1848, April 1997.

[HSI 98] HSIEH M.-H., WEI C.-H., "Channel estimation for OFDM systems based on comb-type pilot arrangement in frequency selective fading channels", *IEEE Transations on Consumer Electronics*, vol. 44, no. 1, pp. 217–225, February 1998.

[IEE 07] IEEE STD 802.11, Wireless LAN medium access control (MAC) and physical layer (PHY) specifications, IEEE, 2007.

[IUT 13] IUTZLER F., CIBLAT P., "Fully distributed signal detection: application to cognitive radio", *EUSIPCO*, Marrakech, Morocco, pp. 1–5, September 2013.

[JAF 00] JAFFROT E., Estimation de canal très sélectif en temps et en fréquence pour les systèmes OFDM, PhD thesis, ENSTA, 2000.

[JOU 11] JOUINI W., "Energy detection limits under log-normal approximated noise uncertainty", *IEEE Signal Processing Letters*, vol. 18, no. 7, pp. 423–426, July 2011.

[KAY 98] KAY S.M., "Algorithm for Estimation", *Fundamentals of Statistical Signal Processing: Detection Theory*, vol. 2, Prentice-Hall, 1998.

[KAY 03a] KAY S.M., "Maximum likelihood estimation", *Fundamentals of Statistical Signal Processing: Estimation Theory*, pp. 157–214, Prentice Hall, 2003.

[KAY 03b] KAY S., *Fundamentals of Statistical Signal Processing: Estimation Theory*, Chapter 12, pp. 388–391, Prentice Hall, 2003.

[KEL 00] KELLER T., HANZO L., "Adaptive multicarrier modulation: a convenient framework for time-frequency processing in wireless communications", *Proceedings of the IEEE*, vol. 88, no. 5, pp. 611–640, May 2000.

[KHA 10] KHALAF Z., NAFKHA A., PALICOT J., *et al.*, "Hybrid spectrum sensing architecture for cognitive radio equipment", *Advanced International Conference on Telecommunications*, pp. 46–51, May 2010.

[KHA 13] KHALAF Z., Contributions à l'étude de détection des bandes libres dans le contexte de la radio intelligente, PhD thesis, Supélec, Rennes, February 2013.

[KHA 14] KHALAF Z., PALICOT J., "New blind free-band detectors exploiting cyclic autocorrelation function sparsity", *Cognitive Communication and Cooperative HetNet Coexistence*, pp. 91–118, Springer, 2014.

[KOS 02] KOSTYLEV V.I., "Energy Detection df a signal with random amplitude", *ICC*, vol. 3, pp. 1606–1610, 2002.

[LE 07] LE SAUX B., Estimation de canal pour système multi-antennes multi-porteuses, PhD thesis, INSA Rennes, 2007.

[LI 02] LI B., FAZIO R.D., ZEIRA A., "A low bias algorithm to estimate negative SNRs in an AWGN channel", *IEEE Communications Letters*, vol. 6, no. 11, pp. 469–471, November 2002.

[LIU 13] LIU F., GUO S., SUN Y., "Primary user signal detection based on virtual multiple antennas for cognitive radio networks", *Progress In Electromagnetics Research C*, vol. 42, pp. 213–227, 2013.

[LU 12] LU L., ZHOU X., ONUNKWO U., *et al.*, "Ten years of research in spectrum sensing and sharing in cognitive radio", *EURASIP Journal on Wireless Communications and Networking*, vol. 2012, no. 28, pp. 1–16, January 2012.

[LUN 07] LUNDÉN J., KOIVUNEN V., HUTTUNEN A., *et al.*, "Spectrum sensing in cognitive radios based on multiple cyclic frequencies", *Crowncom*, Orlando, FL, pp. 37–43, August 2007.

[MA 07] MA J., LI Y., "Soft combination and detection for cooperative spectrum sensing in cognitive radio networks", *GLOBECOM*, Washington, DC, pp. 3139–3143, November 2007.

[MIT 99] MITOLA J., MAGUIRE G.Q., "Cognitive radio: making software radios more personal", *IEEE Personal Communications Magazine*, vol. 6, no. 4, pp. 13–18, August 1999.

[MOR 01] MORELLI M., MENGALI U., "A comparisaon of pilot-aided channel estimation methods for OFDM systems", *IEEE Transactions on Signal Processing*, vol. 49, no. 12, pp. 3065–3073, December 2001.

[NAK 60] NAKAGAMI M., "Statistical methods in radio wave propagation", *The m-Distribution – A General Formula of Intensity Distribution of Rapid Fading*, Symposium Publications Division, Pergamon Press, pp. 3–36, 1960.

[OZD 07] OZDEMIR M.K., ARSLAN H., "Channel estimation for wireless OFDM systems", *IEEE Communications Surveys and Tutorials*, vol. 9, no. 2, pp. 18–48, 2nd Quarter 2007.

[PAT 99] PATZOLD M., *Mobile Fading Channels*, John Wiley & Sons, 1999.

[PAU 00] PAULUZZI D.R., BEAUIEU N.C., "A comparison of SNR estimation techniques for the AWGN channel", *IEEE Transactions on Communications*, vol. 48, no. 10, pp. 1681–1691, October 2000.

[PEL 80] PELED A., RUIZ A., "Frequency domain data transmission using reduced computational complexity algorithms", *ICASSP '80*, vol. 3, pp. 964–967, April 1980.

[PEN 09] PENNA F., GARELLO R., "Theoretical performance analysis of eigenvalue-based detection", *CoRR*, vol. abs/0907.1523, September 2009.

[PRI 61] PRICE R., ABRAMSON N., "Detection theory", *IEEE Transactions on Information Theory*, vol. 7, no. 3, pp. 135–139, July 1961.

[PRO 08] PROAKIS J., SALEHI M., *Digital Communications*, McGraw-Hill, 2008.

[REN 05] REN G., CHANG Y., ZHANG H., "A new SNR's estimator for QPSK modulations in an AWGN channel", *IEEE Transactions on Circuits and Systems*, vol. 52, no. 6, pp. 336–338, June 2005.

[REN 09] REN G., ZHANG H., CHANG Y., "SNR estimation algorithm based on the preamble for OFDM systems in frequency selective channels", *IEEE Transactions on Communications*, vol. 57, no. 8, pp. 2230–2234, August 2009.

[RIC 48] RICE S.O., "Statistical properties of a sine wave plus random noise", *Bell Sytem Technical Journal*, vol. 27, pp. 109–157, 1948.

[SAH 04] SAHAI A., HOVEN N., TANDRA R., "Some fundamental limits on cognitive radio", *Forty-Second Allerton Conference on Communication, Control and Computing*, p. 11, September 2004.

[SAV 12] SAVAUX V., LOUËT Y., DJOKO-KOUAM M., *et al.*, "An iterative and joint estimation of SNR and frequency selective channel for OFDM systems", *European Wireless*, Poznan, Poland, pp. 1–7, April 2012.

[SAV 13a] SAVAUX V., LOUËT Y., DJOKO-KOUAM M., *et al.*, "Application of a joint and iterative MMSE-based estimation of SNR and frequency selective channel for OFDM systems", *EURASIP Journal on Advances in Signal Processing*, no. 1, pp. 1–11, July 2013.

[SAV 13b] SAVAUX V., LOUËT Y., DJOKO-KOUAM M., *et al.*, "Estimation MMSE itérative et conjointe du rapport signal à bruit et du canal sélectif en fréquence pour les systèmes OFDM", *GRETSI*, Brest, France, September 2013.

[SAV 13c] SAVAUX V., LOUËT Y., DJOKO-KOUAM M., *et al.*, "Minimum mean-square-error expression of LMMSE channel estimation in SISO OFDM systems", *IET Electronics Letters*, vol. 49, no. 18, pp. 1152–1154, August 2013.

[SAV 13d] SAVAUX V., Contribution à l'estimation de canal multi-trajets dans un contexte de modulation OFDM, PhD thesis, Supélec, Rennes, France, November 2013.

[SAV 14] SAVAUX V., DJOKO-KOUAM M., LOUËT Y., *et al.*, "Convergence analysis of a joint signal-to-noise ratio and channel estimator for frequency selective channels in orthogonal frequency division multiplexing context", *IET Signal Processing*, 2014.

[SCH 92] SCHOUKENS J., PINTELON R., HAMME H.V., "The Interpolated fast fourier transform: a comparative study", *IEEE Transactions on Instrumentation and Measurement*, vol. 41, no. 2, pp. 226–232, April 1992.

[SCO 99] SCOTT J., "The how and why of COFDM", *EBU Technical Review*, pp. 1–14, January 1999.

[SHE 06] SHEN Y., MARTINEZ E., Channel estimation in OFDM systems, Report, Freescale Semiconductor, 2006.

[SPE 02] SPECTRUM EFFICIENCY WORKING GROUP, Report of the spectrum efficiency working group, Report, Federal Communications Commission, November 2002.

[STE 99] STEENDAM H., MOENECLAEY M., "Analysis and optimization of the performance of OFDM on frequency-selective time-selective fading channels", *IEEE Transactions on Communications*, vol. 47, no. 12, pp. 1811–1819, December 1999.

[SUM 98] SUMMERS T.A., WILSON S.G., "SNR mismatch and online estimation in turbo decoding", *IEEE Transactions on Communications*, vol. 46, no. 4, pp. 421–423, April 1998.

[TAN 05] TANG H., "Some physical layer issues of wide-band cognitive radio systems", *IEEE International Symposium on New Frontiers in Dynamic Spectrum Access Networks*, Baltimore, MD, pp. 151–159, November 2005.

[TAN 08] TANDRA R., SAHAI A., "SNR walls for signal detection", *IEEE Journal of Selected Topics in Signal Processing*, vol. 2, pp. 4–17, February 2008.

[VAN 95] VAN DE BEEK J.J., EDFORS O., SANDELL M., *et al.*, "On channel estimation in OFDM systems", *IEEE conference on Vehicular Technology*, Chicago, IL, vol. 2, pp. 815–819, September 1995.

[WEI 51] WEIBULL W., "A statistical distribution function of wide applicability", *Journal of Applied Mechanics*, vol. 18, pp. 293–297, 1951.

[WIE 06] WIESEL A., ELDAR Y.C., BECK A., "Maximum likelihood estimation in linear models With a Gaussian model matrix", *IEEE Signal Processing Letters*, vol. 13, no. 5, pp. 292–295, May 2006.

[XU 05a] XU H., WEI G., ZHU J., "A novel SNR estimation algorithm for OFDM", *IEEE Vehicular Technology Conference Spring*, vol. 5, pp. 3068–3071, May 2005.

[XU 05b] XU X., JING Y., YU X., "Subspace-based noise variance and SNR estimation for OFDM systems", *IEEE Mobile Radio Applications Wireless Communication Networking Conference*, vol. 1, pp. 23–26, March 2005.

[YÜC 09] YÜCEK T., ARSLAN H., "A survey of spectrum sensing algorithms for cognitive radio applications", *IEEE Communications Surveys and Tutorials*, vol. 11, no. 1, pp. 116–130, 2009.

[YAC 00] YACOUB M.D., "The κ-μ distribution: a general fading distribution", *VTC '00 Fall*, Boston, MA, vol. 2, pp. 872–877, September 2000.

[ZEN 09] ZENG Y., LIANG Y.-C., "Eigenvalue based spectrum sensing algorithms for cognitive radio", *IEEE Transactions on Communications*, vol. 6, no. 57, pp. 1784–1793, June 2009.

Index

Other titles from

in

Waves

BOURLIER Christophe, PINEL Nicolas, KUBICKÉ Gildas
Method of Moments for 2D Scattering Problems: Basic Concepts and Applications

GOURE Jean-Pierre
Optics in Instruments: Applications in Biology and Medicine

LAZAROV Andon, KOSTADINOV Todor Pavlov
Bistatic SAR/GISAR/FISAR Theory Algorithms and Program Implementation

LHEURETTE Eric
Metamaterials and Wave Control

PINEL Nicolas, BOURLIER Christophe
Electromagnetic Wave Scattering from Random Rough Surfaces: Asymptotic models

SHINOHARA Naoki
Wireless Power Transfer via Radiowaves

TERRE Michel, PISCHELLA Mylène, VIVIER Emmanuelle
Wireless Telecommunication Systems

2012

LI Jun-chang, PICART Pascal
Digital Holography

2011

BECHERRAWY Tamer
Mechanical and Electromagnetic Vibrations and Waves
GOURE Jean-Pierre
Optics in Instruments

LE CHEVALIER François, LESSELIER Dominique, STARAJ Robert
Non-standard Antennas

2010

BEGAUD Xavier
Ultra Wide Band Antennas

MARAGE Jean-Paul, MORI Yvon
Sonar and Underwater Acoustics

2009

BOUDRIOUA Azzedine
Photonic Waveguides

BRUNEAU Michel, POTEL Catherine
Materials and Acoustics Handbook

DE FORNEL Frederique, FAVENNEC Pierre-Noël
Measurements using Optic and RF Waves

2008

FILIPPI Paul J.T.
Vibrations and Acoustic Radiation of Thin Structures

2006

BOUCHET Olivier *et al.*
Free-Space Optics

BRUNEAU Michel, SCELO Thomas
Fundamentals of Acoustics

GUILLAUME Philippe
Music and Acoustics

GUYADER Jean-Louis
Vibration in Continuous Media

CPSIA information can be obtained at www.ICGtesting.com
Printed in the USA
BVOW08*1123241014

372149BV00002B/2/P